MURDER
& CRIME

LONDON

MURDER & CRIME

LONDON

PETER DE LORIOL

The
History
Press

For Sophie

First published 2010

The History Press
The Mill, Brimscombe Port
Stroud, Gloucestershire, GL5 2QG
www.thehistorypress.co.uk

© Peter de Loriol, 2010

The right of Peter de Loriol to be identified as the Author
of this work has been asserted in accordance with the
Copyrights, Designs and Patents Act 1988.

British Library Cataloguing in Publication Data.
A catalogue record for this book is available from the British Library.

ISBN 978 0 7524 5657 7

Typesetting and origination by The History Press
Printed in Great Britain
Manufacturing managed by Jellyfish Print Solutions Ltd

CONTENTS

ACKNOWLEDGEMENTS

I would like to thank the London Library, my *Alma Mater*, whose resources are unparalleled, and the British Library, the London Boroughs of Borough, Lambeth, Wandsworth and Westminster Local Studies Libraries for their invaluable assistance. I would also like to thank Sarah Hodgson and Rupert Willoughby for their unstinting support.

I should like to thank Nicola Guy, my publisher, for her help and advice. A belated thanks to Adam Fremantle, my cousin, whose untimely death robbed me of a model of encouragement, and last but not least, my wife, Janey, whose suggestions and editing skills I could not do without.

INTRODUCTION

The sheer brutal savagery of life in London, irrespective of the outwardly prosperous and organised exterior, is reflected in its crimes.

All cities have a larger share of the national crime figures – London is no exception. London's sheer size, diversity and density since the end of the sixteenth-century has given it a pre-eminence in all spheres. Its greatness lies not just in the monstrous powerhouse that it is, but in some of the most sadistic, ferocious and elaborate crimes the world has ever seen.

It is not just the lust for life that created some of the heinous crimes that litter these pages, it is passion in all its colours; greed, jealousy and fear, not forgetting righting a perceived wrong or deep psychological problems.

Some crimes may have been politically motivated, such as the murdered magistrate Sir Edmund Berry Godfrey in the seventeenth-century, or Guy Fawkes' attempt to blow up Parliament. Was one, or both, a deliberate attempt by the Government of the day to garner public opinion? The deliberate City fraud in the early nineteenth-century, did it really warrant an execution? Its results laid the foundations of changes in the law.

Foreigners have been given asylum in Britain, but when a crime was committed, or perceived to have been committed by one, the public and the law demanded satisfaction. Foreigners also add a bit of glamour to the crime, making the public bay for more, as seen in chapter six when a well-turned out Swiss woman – one Mrs Manning – was involved in a murder based on greed and revenge.

Butchered remains were found in two of the most notorious crimes in London history, one of which continues to enthral and disgust the public to this day. The tentacles of the nascent press, eager to make a fortune, fed the voracious appetite of the world by making the unpalatable a drug that one can't do without. One press baron claimed: 'whatever benefits the newspapers is justifiable and it is not my business to consider the effect of their content on the public mind.'

The perfect crime, without bloodshed, would remain a mystery for twenty-five years and its perpetrator would become the darling of the press and the public, while bored middle-class men's proclivities would touch all spheres of society.

The deranged minds of several individuals created a miasma of serial deaths that shocked London and the nation alike, questioning the powers of the police, the establishment, and the very fabric of society.

Crime has no boundaries. It covers all spheres of society, all areas and all methods, from mind games to guns, from knives to poison and gas. The litany of London crimes is immense and this is just a start!

Peter de Loriol, 2010

one

THE WEAPON OF THE WEAK
PRETENDING TO BE STRONG

History, like fashion, is cyclical. Middle England would currently have it that Parliament is riddled with Scotsmen. The Government is highly unpopular. The question of religion is also a hot topic, particularly imported religion. Politics, it seems, never changes.

This was also the case when Elizabeth I died in 1603. There was a debate as to who would succeed. Elizabeth favoured King James VI of Scotland, and accordingly James succeeded Elizabeth I as the closest living relative of the unmarried, childless English monarch, through his descent from one of Henry VIII's sisters. There was no denying that whilst Elizabeth gave England a new sense of identity, a self-confidence and a feeling of sovereignty, people were not altogether sad that she had died. The Tudors had emptied the country's coffers, and whilst it was a newly Protestant country with a strong sense of identity, the Queen had refrained, in her later years, from totally scinding from Catholics, as she had courtiers who were both Catholic and loyal to her. There were, however, very strong penalties for Catholics who openly flouted the laws that banned Mass. James VI of Scotland and I of England was initially seen as a breath of fresh air . . .

Unfortunately, James I, possibly the most intellectual, and certainly the most open-minded British monarch, had other ideas that were anathema to English hearts, specifically Catholic English hearts. He transported his Scottish Court to London, bestowing honours and power to his Scottish favourites.

The Scots were openly derided and almost universally hated by Parliament and the people. They were 'an effusion of people from Northern parts'. The Scots were also considered uncouth, filthy, lousy and jeered at because of their accent. There was also talk in Parliament of 'plants which are transported from barren ground into a more fertile one and how they grow and overgrow'. King James, furthermore, committed the cardinal sin of suggesting that the entire island should be known as 'Britain' – this met with the most disgusted response.

Catholics who thought there might be some change for the better were swiftly disillusioned with the escalation of fines on the Catholic recusants. Fines, totaling an average of £3,500 per year, rose to epic proportions by 1604 – so draconian were these that many saw their estates sequestered and were reduced to penury. Some of these estates were then given, by Royal largesse, to the 'parvenu' Scots! It was as a result of such laws, the new monarch and his Scottish favourites that the 'Gunpowder Plot' was supposedly hatched.

Robert Catesby, son of a distinguished Catholic line, was related to other distinguished Catholic families, the Treshams, Throckmortons, Vaux, and Wintours – Midland gentry.

His cousin had also married Lord Monteagle, a powerful personage at Court. Catesby was a bright, attractive man, with exceptional ability to command and much admired by many of his contemporaries. Unfortunately this gentle, emotional man's Protestant wife died early, leaving him directionless. He reverted to extreme Catholicism and was heavily involved with the Earl of Essex's abortive coup in 1601. His recklessness lost him a fortune. By being labeled a rebel he had to forfeit his estate. This led him down the path of Catholic theology and towards the idea of a new Catholic State. The overriding problem in the eyes of most English Catholics was that whilst Elizabeth I was considered illegitimate, James I had rightfully acceded to the throne. Any action against the 'rightful king' would contradict the loyalties of the rest of the English Catholics.

On 20 May 1604, a group of people assembled at the Duck and Drake Inn in the Strand. Robert Catesby summoned Tom Wintour (Winter), Jack (John) Wright, Thomas Percy and Guido Fawkes. His scheme was simple – to blow up Parliament House when the King and his Parliament would be in residence. He believed he had tried all other means to make the Catholics be heard, but now the King must be called to account as he had a contractual obligation towards his people. Princess Elizabeth, furthermore, would be abducted and placed as a titular queen. He and other Catholics had tried to enlist the help of Catholic Spain, but despite the fancy Spanish rhetoric, Spain had promised but not donated funds, nor had Spain promised any military support. Spain, in the wake of a very expensive war and a failed campaign in Ireland, was ultra cautious. They had, however, managed to inveigle Guido (Guy) Fawkes, a Catholic Yorkshireman, a captain in Sir William Stanley's mercenary troops presently in the pay of Spain, and an expert in gunpowder.

Unlike the others, Guy Fawkes was not related to any of them, but had been to school with Jack Wright and had met Thomas Wintour in 1603 in Spain. Both men had been sent there secretly by an Englishman living on the Continent. This Englishman remains unknown to this day and is only referred to as the 'Caballero Ingles' by Spanish sources. Both had actively tried to galvanise the Court of King Philip to supply arms, soldiers and money to assist the Catholics in England, but nothing had come of it. Fawkes, fluent in both French and Spanish, was far more of a nationalist than simply pro-Catholic. He told the Spanish that:

…there is a natural hostility between the English and the Scots. There has always been one, and at present it keeps increasing through these grievances, so that even were there but one religion in England it would not be possible to reconcile these two nations, as they are, for very long.

Guido Fawkes.

The plotters had a lucky break in 1604. Thomas Percy was appointed a Gentleman Pensioner in June. This meant that he needed to have quarters near Parliament. He chose a small apartment in the precincts of Westminster, John

The conspirators.

Whynniard's house. Fawkes was placed as caretaker under the assumed name of John Johnson, servitor to Mr Percy.

That summer was a tense time for Catholics. Anti-Catholic legislation was pushed through Parliament and priests were put to death. The autumn brought no solace as recusant fines were back in full force and James I asked Lord Ellesmere to 'exterminate priests and other corrupt people'. Parliament's adjournment enabled the plotters to regroup in the country, returning in October with a new member, Robert Keyes. Robert Keyes would be the one to arrange for gunpowder to be stored at Catesby's house on the Lambeth shores.

Gunpowder was now relatively easy to obtain as the previous monarch's wars had made the Council encourage home production of gunpowder and the new Anglo-Spanish peace meant that there was a glut of it. There were several gunpowder factories around London and a little subterfuge could always supply the requisite amount. Catesby's manservant, Robert Bates, was to join them in December 1604. They were now seven-strong and preparing for action when Parliament returned in February 1605.

The official New Year, 25 March 1605, heralded three new plotters; Robert Wintour, John Grant and Kit Wright, bringing the total to ten. It was also the date when a lease was secured on a cellar directly under the House of Lords, close to Whynniard's house. A total of thirty-six barrels of gunpowder were eventually ferried to the cellar in the ensuing months. Secrecy was paramount, as was military and financial aid. Fawkes was sent back to the Continent, to return by August, and was detected by the Earl of Salisbury's spy network. The network also picked up Catesby's name.

A secret shared is a secret no more, and the larger the group, the greater the risk. Certainly wives would have had a notion of what was going on. Priests accustomed to taking confessions would also hear the unthinkable. A chance indiscretion by a close female relative alerted the possibility of some plot to the Government and the further indiscretions of two priests, Fathers Garnett and Greenaway, applied more pressure.

The gunpowder in the cellars.

Fears over the plague resulted in a setback for the plotters as Parliament prorogued its return until October 1605.

By October 1605 Catesby had recruited three more to the ranks; Ambrose Rookwood, Francis Tresham and Sir Everard Digby. Digby and Rookwood were by far the youngest plotters. It was also in October that the final preparations were made; Fawkes was to light a long enough fuse to allow him to flee before the explosion, there would be an uprising in the Midlands and Princess Elizabeth would be secured.

On 26 October Lord Monteagle received an anonymous letter asking him not to attend Parliament as it was to suffer a horrible blow. Monteagle decided to show the letter to Salisbury, who sat on it and waited.

The 'Monteagle letter' has been a source of contention ever since. Was it a letter from someone close to the plotters but who didn't know the exact plot? Was it from one of the plotters, some of whom were related to Monteagle? Why did Salisbury sit on it – to ensnare the plotters further or to wait for the King's decision? Or was it a concoction by the Government, who knew what the plotters were up to and wanted to ensure good termination to this episode? There is no doubt that Salisbury had more than an inkling of what was going on and a quick end would mean an end to any Catholic unrest in England. This last theory does hold more water than the others.

On Monday, 4 November 1605, a first search of the cellars surrounding Westminster was made by Lords Suffolk and Monteagle. Apart from a surprisingly large amount of firewood in Whynniard's cellar, Whynniard informed them that the current tenant was Thomas Percy. A second search was made in the small hours of 5 November, when a tall man answering to the name of John Johnson was apprehended and kegs of gunpowder discovered. The Government had one name, Thomas Percy.

John Johnson turned out to be Guy Fawkes. He steadfastly maintained that the plot was to blow the Scots back to Scotland. His torture was to elicit more names. Meanwhile, Londoners lit their very first bonfires in celebration of the averted disaster.

By the evening of 6 November, the Government had all the names save Bates, Robert Wintour and Digby, but not through the intransigent, brave and mysterious Fawkes. He did crack – two days later. The rest fled to Holbeche House on the Staffordshire border where Catesby, the two Wrights and Thomas Percy were all fatally wounded by the Sheriff

my lord out of the loue i beare ████ to some of youere frendz
i haue a caer of youer preseruacion therfor i would
aduyse yowe as youe tender youer lyf to deuys some
epscuse to shift of youer attendance at this parleament
for god and man hathe concurred to punishe the wickedues
of this tyme and thinke not slightly eof this aduertisment
but retyere youre self into youre contri wheare youe
maye expect the euent in safti for thowghe theare be no
apparance of anni stir yet i saye they shall receyue a terrible
blowe this parleament and yet they shall not seie who
hurts them this coumcel is not to be a contemned becaus
it maye do youe good and can do youe no harme for the
dangere is passed as soon as youe haue burnt the letter
and i hope god will giue youe the grace to mak good
use of it to whose holy proteccion i commend youe

Inscribed on the back.

To the ryght honorable
the Lord mowteagle

The Monteagle letter.

of Worcester's men on 8 November. Robert and Thomas Wintour managed to escape, but were eventually found. Francis Tresham died in the Tower of London.

On January 27 1606, Digby, Robert Wintour, John Grant, Thomas Bates, Thomas Wintour, Ambrose Rookwood, Robert Keyes and Guy Fawkes were summarily tried. None denied treason and all were condemned to be executed.

The execution of the conspirators.

On Thursday 30 January, Digby, Robert Wintour, John Grant and Thomas Bates were hanged in St Paul's churchyard, then drawn and quartered. Thomas Wintour, Ambrose Rookwood, Robert Keyes and Guy Fawkes met the same fate the next day in the Old Palace Yard at Westminster.

The unpopular government took full advantage of this 'evil' plot. It even concocted a story that the conspirators had dug a mine (which was never discovered) from December 1604 and October 1605 between the rented apartments and Parliament – a beautifully crafted piece of political sleight-of-hand that would encapsulate the evilness of The Wrongdoers and spice up the 'account' of the averted danger.

The question remains, why was Francis Tresham, cousin of Monteagle, alone sent to the Tower, unlike the others? He died of natural causes – or was it poison, administered by himself or by someone else who didn't want him to talk? There is some evidence that he may have been the one who named names . . .

two

A MAN OF PROBITY

The late seventeenth century was riddled with political fears. England had just come out of a period of enforced austerity under the Cromwells and had been catapulted back to the Franco-Scottish Court of the Stuart dynasty with its plethora of French and Scottish adventurers and its European intrigues. The English had a natural abhorrence of the foreigner, let alone of the French. Their real fear, however, was of the Catholic faith that seemed to permeate the Court circles and the upper echelons of English society, threatening the very fabric of that society. The following murder encapsulates all these fears and remains unsolved to this day.

In the early evening of 17 October 1678, two regulars of the White House Inn at Lower Chalcott (present day Chalk Farm), accompanied by the landlord, the constable of the

Chalk Farm.

parish of Marylebone and a group of others, walked to a drainage ditch on the south side slope of Primrose Hill. There, among the brambles, lay the body of a man of substance, face down, a sword run through the body and his coat thrown over his head. His belongings were strewn about the ground.

The body, sword withdrawn, was carried back to the inn and the authorities informed. It was only then that the body was identified as Sir Edmund Berry Godfrey, knight, late magistrate of the King and a successful City merchant.

On Friday 18 October the Coroner of Middlesex, John Cooper, empanelled a jury at the White House Inn. Sir Edmund's brother, Michael, and two surgeons, Zachariah Skillard and Cambridge, were in attendance. The surgeons' evidence created questions rather than answered them:

> His sword was thrust through him, but no blood was on his clothes or about him; his shoes were clean; his money was in his pocket, but nothing was about his neck (although when he went from home, he had a large lace band on), and a mark was all around it, an inch broad, which showed he had been strangled. His breast was likewise all over marked with bruises, and his neck was broken; and it was visible he was first strangled, then carried to that place, where his sword was run through his dead body.

The ditch was dry – no blood marks in it – his shoes were clean and everything but his pocket book was found. The pocket book was one he used as a magistrate. Spots of white wax, an item he never used, but used by noblemen and priests, were scattered over his clothes.

The conclusion was that he had been killed by Roman Catholics. His murder would prove a very useful tool for the bigot, the scaremonger and the state!

Edmund Berry Godfrey (1621-1678) was one of eighteen children of a prominent Kent family. His career in London followed the usual pattern of the younger sons – trade or a profession. He followed law, but then chose to go into business as a wood and coal merchant, with premises in Green Lane (beneath Charing Cross Station) then in Hartshorn Lane (Northumberland Avenue) and various properties including the Swan Tavern in King Street, Hammersmith. He was made a Justice of the Peace for the Court quarter of London. His conduct during the Great Plague in 1664-5 (in one instance, on the refusal of his men to enter a pest-house to apprehend a man who had stolen winding sheets from the dead to re-sell, he went in himself and arrested him) earned him a knighthood. He was a respected magistrate who had had plans for the beggars of London – he was to set them to work!

Godfrey, although an Anglican, was known for his moderate views, and was friends to Anglicans and Catholics alike. He mixed in the Court circles and was known to the Lord Treasurer Lord Danby.

Sir Edmund Berry Godfrey.

He had last been seen alive some time after 2 p.m. on 12 October, in the fields near the White House on Primrose Hill – a walk he was known to take on a regular basis. Another sighting had placed Godfrey in the Strand and Lincoln's Inn. What was definitely known was that Godfrey was frightened for himself after the swearing of secret documents shown to him by a certain Dr Titus Oates, and he had left his home early on 12 October.

The Roman Catholic problem was a very real one; that is, in the minds of the people. The fear of Roman Catholicism was founded on the sixteenth-century Elizabeth's accession and the defeat of the Armada, with the added bonus of the 1605 Gunpowder Plot. Roman Catholics were deemed to be capable of any action to reinstall Roman Catholicism in England, not helped by a very tolerant atmosphere at Court. Added to which there was a high proportion of Catholics in London, freedom of worship and the fact that James Duke of York, a Catholic convert, openly expressed his religious beliefs.

Titus Oates.

'Doctor' Titus Oates was a very strange man indeed. He was the son of a Protestant preacher who openly detested him. He was physically repellent: he had convulsions, a runny nose and slavered at the mouth. He had a limp, a red face, a bull neck and an enormous chin. His harsh, loud voice was perfect for preaching, and this he did in his craving for acceptance, with a very liberal dose of fantasy added. His life had been one of a fight against the natural repulsion people felt on seeing him and the very real need for his few talents to be recognised. One talent was convincing people, in this particular case convincing them of the power of Roman Catholicism, a fear which his spurious doctorate in divinity coupled with the assistance of Dr Israel Tonge, ensured he would have his fifteen minutes of fame!

Oates and Tonge had been trying to convince Court officials that there was a very real danger from the Catholics. Their premise was that there was a 'Popish Plot' which included murdering the King and replacing him with the Duke of York, the murder of the entire Privy Council, the wholesale massacre of Protestants, and a French invasion of Ireland. The Treasurer, Lord Danby and the Secretary of State, Sir Joseph Williamson, had refused to see them, and to have their 'plot' brought out into the open they had to have their deposition sworn by a magistrate. A man of probity, with Court connections, was Sir Edmund Berry Godfrey. It took them a few days to convince the magistrate that there was indeed a very real danger. Godfrey duly took their sworn statements. He also confided in his Catholic friend Edward Coleman, a servitor to the Duke of York. The Duke then insisted that the Privy Council know of this.

The Privy Council summoned the fabricators of the Popish Plot on 27 September. Neither Danby nor York attended, which was a pity as they would have voiced some reason at the proceedings. The guards were doubled at the palace and Oates, rewarded

The murder of Sir Edmund Berry Godfrey at Somerset House.

with £40 per month, was charged with rooting out the perpetrators of this fiendish plot. Godfrey was conveniently murdered and warrants were issued for the arrest of twenty-six innocent people, who were imprisoned in the Tower and executed. The innocent magistrate, it was rumoured, had been lured to Somerset House on the pretext of stopping a quarrel, strangled with his twisted kerchief, then skewered with his sword by a Jesuit and transported to the suitably remote Primrose Hill.

Godfrey's murder has never been satisfactorily explained; was it the Catholics or Oates' supporters who killed him because he knew it was a fabrication, or the Whigs because they understood how much Godfrey knew about the plot, or even suicide? Another possible contender is Philip Herbert, Earl of Pembroke, who might have taken his revenge for having been prosecuted for murder some time earlier by Godfrey.

A £500 reward was offered for any information, and, on the strength of the statement of a Catholic goldsmith, Miles Prance, and an ex-serviceman, William Bledloe, three clerks at Somerset House – Green, Berry and Hill – were arrested, tried and executed, despite their protestations of innocence.

Godfrey, meanwhile, was buried in state. His body was carried by eight knights, all JPs, and was followed by all the City aldermen and seventy-two clergymen to St Martin's Church to be buried. A tablet to his memory was erected in the east cloister of Westminster Abbey.

Medals commemorating the magistrate's death.

three

HE THAT SHEDDETH MAN'S BLOOD, BY MAN SHALL HIS BLOOD BE SHED

England has witnessed one regicide and one assassination of a Prime Minister. The Chief Minister of the Crown was only officially called 'Prime Minister' from the early twentieth century. Until then the Crown's first Minister was the First Lord of the Treasury and was only called 'Prime Minister' as a joke by colleagues.

Just before quarter past five on the afternoon of Monday, 11 May 1812, the MP William Smith had stopped to speak to a colleague in the half-empty lobby of the House of Commons when he heard a shot in the room. A crowd of people swarmed by the door as a man, clutching his left breast, tottered towards Smith and crashed to the floor. Smith called for help and he and another lifted the man up, only recognising him as he did so. It was Mr Spencer Perceval, the First Lord of the Treasury.

Perceval (1762–1812) was a younger son of a large brood and a lawyer by training. He had an acute mind hampered by the fact that he opposed Catholic emancipation and the reform of Parliament. A devout Christian and family man (he had twelve children), Perceval was to head an unpopular and weak ministry from 1809 until his death, and pursued the Peninsula War to a successful end.

Together, Smith and his colleague carried the diminutive Perceval into the Speaker's secretary's office, laying him on the desk, his feet on two chairs. Perceval made a few gasps and was dead within minutes. Mr William Lynn, a surgeon, checked for any signs of life, also looking for the wound. A large, almost bloodless hole was found

Perceval being shot.

just above Perceval's left breast. The shot had pierced his heart.

Henry Burgess, a solicitor, was also in the lobby. On hearing the shot from the entrance he too had seen Spencer Perceval, clutching his breast, stagger to one of the pillars, mouth something and fall backwards. Cries and fingers pointed to a man sitting on a bench, ashen-faced and shaking, his right hand holding a pistol. Burgess walked towards him and calmly took the still-warm pistol from him. He then asked the murderer why he had done this. The laconic answer was that the man had been ill-used and wanted a redress of grievance from the Government. After a brief pause, Burgess asked the man if he had another pistol about his person and when he answered yes another at the scene, Lieutenant General Isaac Gascoyne, who seemed to know the man, searched his pockets and took another loaded pistol out, as well as a sheaf of papers

Smith comes to the assistance of Mr Perceval.

tied up in a red ribbon. The papers were taken by another MP, Joseph Hume.

The Leader of the House of Commons was dead! The perpetrator was held until Bow Street Runners arrived to take him to Newgate. What, though, had made this well-dressed man of obvious education take the life of another, let alone Spencer Perceval?

The assassin was John Bellingham, of 9 New Milman Street. Nothing was yet known about him except for his grievances against the current administration. The Bow Street Runner, John Vickrey, was dispatched to his address to search the premises. He found a pair of pistol bags, a small powder flask, a pistol key and a quantity of letters and papers (among them a receipt for two half-inch calibre pistols purchased from W. Beckwith, gunsmith of Skinner Street on 20 April), as well as a mould and some balls that fitted the pistols in custody. The papers taken by Lieutenant General Gascoyne also gave an idea as to why the man had resorted to such an extreme measure.

The urgency of the matter dictated that the trial and sentence be carried out with the least of delays. The trial was set for Wednesday 13 May before Sir James Mansfield, Chief Justice of the Common Pleas, the Attorney General William Garrow and the Marquis Wellesley.

John Bellingham explained his reasons for killing Perceval:

… if I am the man that I am supposed to be, to go and deliberately shoot Mr Perceval
without malice, I should consider myself a monster, and not fit to live in this world

John Bellingham.

or the next; the unfortunate lot had fallen upon him as the leading member of that administration which had repeatedly refused me any reparation for the unparalleled injuries I had sustained in Russia for eight years with the cognizance and sanction of the minister of the country at the court of St Petersburg.

It was, he claimed, in 1804 that this 'unhappy affair' started, when he was sent to Russia on business. He took his young pregnant wife with him. A Russian ship, the *Soleure*, was lost in the White Sea and the underwriters at Lloyds, advised by an anonymous letter that the ship was deliberately sunk, refused to pay the owners. The rankled owners, suspicious that Bellingham was the instigator of the letter and aware that he was a guarantor of one of their debtors, accused him of the debt. He was refused an exit pass on the strength of this and the embittered ship owner convinced the local Governor, the Governor of Archangel, to have him imprisoned.

Bellingham petitioned the British Consul and the then British Ambassador, Lord Granville Leveson Gower. The Governor refused to have him freed as he was imprisoned for a legal reason and could not, or would not, pursue this matter further. Bellingham was shunted from prison to prison for two years, enduring privations unimaginable in England, until he managed to gain freedom on his own cognizance. During this time his wife returned to England.

Once free he got a judgement of false imprisonment against the Governor, without the assistance of the British authorities, but was subsequently accused of an alleged 2,000 roubles debt. This he refuted because acceptance would mean imprisonment. He was imprisoned instead for being an alleged bankrupt.

The Russian laws dictated that a bankrupt could be discharged if creditors did not apply for restitution within eighteen months. This was the case for Bellingham. He was then handed over to the College of Commerce and advised that he still owed the 2,000 roubles. Despite representation, the British Consul and the British Ambassador both said they were powerless to help and suggested he should pay the money. This he refused on the grounds that he had never owed it!

On the arrival of the Marquis of Douglas in Russia, Bellingham asked him to intercede on his behalf. Unfortunately, the only effect this had was that the Russian authorities asked him to either pay the full amount or a token amount to admit culpability. This he couldn't do as to admit culpability would be to admit the case against the Governor of Archangel to be false and to admit his debt to the shipping company that had started the whole matter.

His bitterness towards the British authorities in Russia was exacerbated by the successful representation of a British captain of a merchant ship who had been asked for a large bribe by a local Russian captain, and refused. The British Ambassador had successfully interceded on behalf of the British captain. Why couldn't the British authorities do the same for him?

Eventually he was granted leave to go in 1809 and returned to England to demand some compensation from the British Government. His family had pleaded with him to let the matter drop. He started work in London, at the same time making representations to the government. He had even been advised by a civil servant that he could take whatever measure he thought proper!

Unfortunately, the British Government had broken off diplomatic relations with Russia in 1808. He concluded with:

> I laid a statement of my grievances before the Marquis Wellesley, accompanied by authentic documents, and claiming some redress for the injuries I had sustained through the British minister in Russia, which injuries it was impossible I should have suffered, if they had not been sanctioned by that minister. The Marquis is now in Court, and could contradict my statement if false, but I represent the circumstances as they really were and not as personally concerning myself but as involving the honour of the British Government. I was referred by the Marquis to the Privy Council, and from the Privy Council to the Treasury; and thus baffled from one party to another, I applied to Mr Perceval, during the session 1811, but received for answer, from his secretary, that the time for presenting private petitions was gone by, and that Mr Perceval could not encourage my hopes, that he would recommend my claims to the House of Commons.

This left him with no other alternative.

Despite the defence entering a plea of insanity, backed up by witnesses but not supported by the accused, the jury, after fourteen minutes of deliberation, pronounced him guilty. Bellingham was hanged in public on 18 May. He apologised to the crowd beforehand and his body, as was the custom for murderers, was handed over to surgeons for dissection.

The Maréchal de Camp, René-Martin Pillet, a prisoner of war attending the execution, claimed that the assembled crowd said:

> farewell poor man, you owe satisfaction to the laws of your country, but God bless you! You have rendered an important service to your country, you have taught ministers that they should do justice, and grant audience when it is asked of them.

While this is an admirable sentiment, there is some doubt it was ever said, as Pillet was an Anglophobe to the core!

four

MONEY, MONEY, MONEY

In 1800 England, 200 crimes were punishable by death. The progressive democratisation of society put pressure on successive governments to abolish the death penalty, let alone reduce the amount of crimes punishable by death. Several notable persons of the age questioned this seeming callousness of the justice system. One of these was Jeremy Bentham, the philanthropist. The crime of fraud was one of those that earned the death sentence. The following story is an example of this.

The London Bank of Marsh, Sibbald & Co., of Berners Street, was a respected, middling size one. It had been set up in 1792 by William Marsh, a victualler and naval agent, and James (later Sir James) Sibbald of Sittwood Park, Berkshire. The managing partner, once clerk of Barclays, was William Fauntleroy, a respected and upstanding City merchant. They were joined in 1796 By Mr (later Sir) Josias Stracey, husband of Sibbald's niece.

Fauntleroy's son, Henry, became a clerk at the bank in 1800 and upon his father's unexpected death, aged 57, in 1807, he was offered a partnership.

Henry Fauntleroy (1784-1824) was neat, elegant and industrious – he inspired confidence. He was, moreover, charming and friendly with a supreme belief in himself. His ego was such that he often likened himself to his hero Napoleon Bonaparte, whose bust he kept on the mantelpiece in the family home next to the bank. Within a short time Fauntleroy became the only working partner in the business and virtual master of financing.

The bank lent money to building contractors, mostly in Marylebone. The state of the country's finances following the Napoleonic Wars hit the City and its banking houses, one of which was Marsh, Sibbald & Co. To shore up the finances of the business and prove his integrity, Fauntleroy married Susannah Young in 1809, daughter of John Young, a naval officer and landowner in St Kitts. A son was born shortly afterwards. The marriage lasted barely a year.

The young businessman then plunged into a series of expensive affairs with high-class prostitutes such as 'Mrs Bang', otherwise known as Miss Kent, and the infamous Harriet Wilson. Much of his time was spent in his splendid villa in Brighton. He took up with Maria Forbes in 1819 and settled her in Lambeth – he had two children by her.

The losses on advances to developers amounted to £60,000 in 1810, covered by the Bank of England. A further £100,000 losses caused Fauntleroy to adopt desperate measures, especially when the Bank of England refused Marsh, Sibbald & Co.'s acceptances in 1815, at a time when that Bank was totally committed to the financing of development of the Portman Estate in Marylebone and was in dire financial straits.

23

Clients placed shares and securities with Marsh, Sibbald & Co. Fauntleroy hit on the idea of forging Powers of Attorney for navy loans, annuities and consols (government bonds/annuities) and selling them at the Bank of England, but dividends were paid to the owners and entered into the bank's ledgers. His eventual fraud amounted to around £360,000. He was always worried he would be found out – there were some narrow escapes! He was at the Bank of England once, handling a Power of Attorney to a clerk when the owner of the stock came in. He stopped the transaction and walked out with the victim.

In September 1824, J.D. Hulme, a custom house official and trustee of an estate with Marsh, Sibbald & Co., visited the Bank of England only to find £10,000 in consols missing. The stock had been sold by Marsh, Sibbald & Co. with Fauntleroy forging the trustees' signatures. Freshfield, the Bank of England solicitor, arranged a warrant for the arrest of Fauntleroy.

Early in the morning of 10 September, PC Samuel Plante arrested Fauntleroy as he walked into the bank. He was immediately committed to Coldbath Prison. The bank stopped trading, a police court examination on 18 September ensured that he was charged and sent to Newgate Prison on the 19th. Accusations and gossip maintained that Fauntleroy had lived beyond his means and had been profligate with his clients' money – accusations seized on and embellished by the papers. There was no doubt that he had misappropriated funds for Marsh, Sibbald & Co.'s benefit, and also for his own pleasures.

The trial was held on 30 September at a packed Old Bailey. The entrance fee was one guinea. James Harmer was the solicitor for the defence and John Gurney the barrister. Justice Park, Baron Garrow and the Attorney General Sir John Copley presided.

Henry Fauntleroy's professionalism convicted him. A box found in Berners Street had his confession, dated 7 July 1816:

In order to keep up the credit of our house I have forged powers of attorney, and have thereupon sold out all these sums, without the knowledge of my partners. I have given

James Harmer, Fauntleroy's defence lawyer.   Henry Fauntleroy in the dock.

credit for the accounts when the interest became due. The Bank of England began first to refuse our acceptances, and thereby destroy the credits of our house; they shall smart for this.

Ever the diligent clerk, he also made a ledger of the fraudulent transactions, footnoted with:

…in order to keep up the credit of our house, I have forged powers of attorney for the above sums and parties, and sold out to the amount here stated, and without the knowledge of my partners. I kept up the payments of the dividends, but made no entries of such payments in our books.

The jury took fifteen minutes to reach a verdict – Guilty. The sentence of death was pronounced on 2 November and despite the case being argued twice on points of law before judges and petitions presented to the Home Secretary, Robert Peel, Fauntleroy was hanged before a huge crowd outside Newgate Prison on 30 November 1824.

Fauntleroy was the last forger to hang in England, as capital punishment for forgery was abolished in 1832.

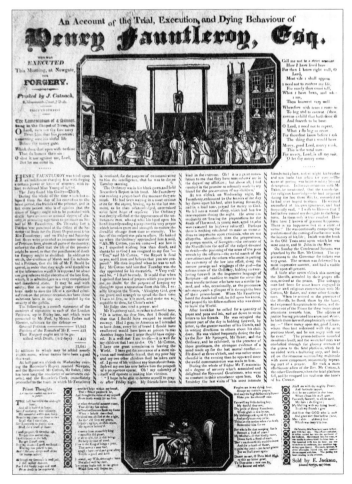

A newspaper account of Fauntleroy's execution.

five

HONESTY IS THE BEST POLICY

The early 1800s saw a massive shift in population to the cities as whole village communities sought work in the progressively industrialised towns. London was no exception. In 1801 it had a population of just under a million and by the middle of the century that had doubled.

The immediate surroundings of the West End were the first to be built up by the developers, with large estates such as the Portman estate being developed and the gradual urbanisation of the land adjacent to the Edgware Road. The public house, the Hero of Maida, was opened shortly after the Battle of Maida in Southern Italy in 1806 and the area began to be developed, with a string of select houses and villas that were to become the suburb of Maida Vale. The area, though, retained its rural atmosphere with stag hunts continuing to at least 1829. In the same year, the entrepreneur George Shillibeer introduced a French invention, the omnibus, on to the new road from Paddington to the City.

In the mid-1830s a new row of detached houses, Canterbury Villas, was built across from Edgware Road, from Pineapple Place parallel to what is now Sutherland Avenue. This quiet, leafy area was ideal for the emerging professional classes. Its very seclusion, though, was the stage for the most blood-curdling crime of the century – that is until Jack the Ripper.

At about midday on a cold 28 December 1836, a labourer, Robert Bond, was walking to work via the Pineapple Toll Gate when he spied a large hessian sack tied up at the top outside one of the Canterbury villas. Intrigued, he opened the sack and recoiled in horror, for inside was the torso of a woman. PC Samuel Pegler of 'S' Division was walking his beat when the breathless Bond rushed up to him, explained what he had found and took him back to the sack.

The torso was conveyed to Paddington police station in Hermitage Street, sealed in vinegar and an inquest was held at the White Lion Inn, Edgware Road. There were no identifying marks and despite extensive newspaper coverage no one came forward. 'Wilful Murder against a person or persons unknown', however, was established. One potential clue lay in the wood shavings and rags at the bottom of the bag.

It was not until 6 January 1837 that the papers had more to report. On that day a bargeman, 'Berkham Bob' Tomlin, was trying to close the Ben Johnson lock gates on one of the stretches of the Regent's Canal near Stepney. They just wouldn't budge. He and the lock-keeper used a hitcher (a long pole with a hook at the end) to remove the obstruction. Finally they managed to dislodge it and pulled the pole up to find a woman's head with only one eye, a fractured jawbone and a slit ear, perched at the end!

The head was brought back to Paddington police station where the police surgeon, Mr Girdwood, examined both torso and head, determining that the head and trunk were part of the same body. It was preserved in alcohol and put on display for people to see. The papers advertised the fact, just in case a member of the public might recognise it.

Where the railway now runs between Shakespeare Road and Hinton Road in Brixton was then covered in osier fields. On Thursday 2 February, a young man was cutting osiers in Mr Tenpenney's field when he discovered a large, filled hessian sack. He opened it to find the remains of human thighs and legs. Once again the remains were carted to Paddington police station, where it was determined that the legs belonged to the head and torso already there. Some wood shavings were also found at the bottom of this bag.

Mrs William Gay of Goodge Street followed the newspaper reports like everyone else. She, however, on reading that the ear on the head was torn, became convinced that this was her missing sister-in-law, Mrs Hannah Brown. Mrs Brown had disappeared a week before her wedding, on 25 December 1836, to the affluent Mr James Greenacre of Lambeth.

Mrs Gay convinced her husband, William, to go and view the head. He did, and recognised the slit ear, as did friends of theirs. The police took statements from all those who had come into contact with Mrs Brown.

Hannah Brown had been a handsome 45-year-old washerwoman who lived in Union Street, by Middlesex Hospital. Twice married and now single, she had put aside, so she had claimed, about £400, a goodly amount. She was to marry James Greenacre on Christmas day at St Giles-in-the-Fields, with Mr Davis, cabinet maker of 45 Bartholomew Close, Smithfield, giving her away. The Davises had last seen an agitated Mr Greenacre, with a bag under his arm, on Christmas Eve. He had explained that Mrs Brown had lied to him about her affairs and the wedding was off.

A Mrs Glass of Windmill Street, Tottenham Court Road, had waited for her friend Mrs Brown on that same evening but she had never arrived – which was curious, because she was due to stay the night. A well-dressed middle-aged man had knocked on another of Mrs Brown's friends' door, Mrs Blanchard, on 27 December, and told her that the wedding was off because Mrs Brown had tried to purchase goods in a tally-shop in his name. Not only that, but she had 'grossly imposed on him' and had lied about her circumstances. This man, Mr Greenacre, had then been introduced to her tenant, Mrs Gay, wife of Mrs Brown's estranged brother. Mr Greenacre had promptly left.

Inspector Feltham was placed in charge of the investigation. The only person who could account for Hannah's last actions was her fiancé, James Greenacre of Lambeth. A warrant for the arrest of Mr Greenacre was issued on 26 March, although it took a little while to find out his exact whereabouts – which turned out to be 1 St Albans Place, Lambeth.

Mr Greenacre initially told the officers he knew of no Mrs Hannah Brown. He then conceded that he was to have married a certain Mrs Brown, and had they arrived the next day they would not have found him as he would have sailed for America! The packed trunks in his room seemed to prove this. The young woman found sharing his bed attempted to conceal something in her hands. Feltham ordered her to give him what she was hiding: a watch, two rings and a pair of earrings. Miss Sarah Gale was then asked to dress, and they were both placed under arrest. She collected her child from the adjoining room and they and the packed trunks were conveyed to Paddington police station.

On inspection, it appeared that some of the clothes in the trunks seemed to be very similar to the rags found in the first hessian sack, and some of the articles belonged to the

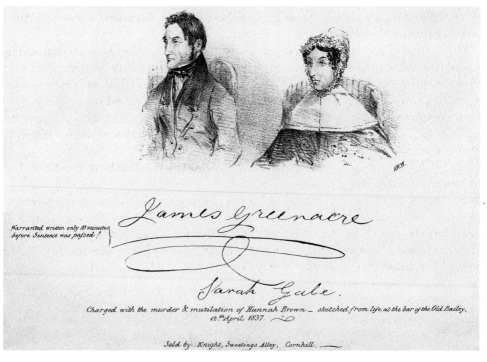

James Greenacre and Sarah Gale at the Old Bailey.

dead woman, including those taken from Miss Gale. The sacks belonged to a Mr Ward, cabinet maker of Tottenham Court Road and the man who had introduced Mr Greenacre to Mrs Brown. The wood shavings proved this.

The desperate Greenacre tried to hang himself but was promptly revived and the suspects were taken by coach to the magistrates' court on Marylebone Road. At the hearing Greenacre admitted that he had given Sarah Gale notice to quit before Hannah Brown's arrival. Mrs Brown had arrived with her boxes on Christmas Eve a little worse for wear and picked a quarrel with Greenacre. He found out that she had used his name to obtain credit and in a temper he tipped her chair back, knocking her head against a wooden beam. He tried to revive her but couldn't. He panicked, sawed her body up and deposited the pieces in various parts of London. He admitted that he had wrapped her head in a silk handkerchief and calmly carried it on his knee as he rode on a London omnibus on his way to the Regent's Canal. He had been carrying her head when he had visited Mrs Davis.

The police surgeons, however, maintained that Mrs Brown's eye was dislodged when she had either been hit or fallen very heavily. They also said that she had been quartered alive.

Their trial was set for 10 April at the Old Bailey. Lord Chief Justice Tindal, Mr Justice Coleridge and Mr Justice Coltman presided.

By then it was established that Greenacre had had a chequered life and was a serial widower. He had first been a grocer in Southwark, became an overseer of the parish and married a daughter of the landlord of the Crown and Anchor Tavern in Woolwich. She died of a fever. He then married a Miss Romford and had seven children by her, but four of them died, and so did his wife. His third marriage was to a propertied widow, whose dowry brought him a series of properties on Bowyers Lane (between Camberwell Road and Camberwell New Road).

His business prospered until greed got the better of him. He dabbled in untaxed tea but was discovered by the Excise. He opted to leave for America with his youngest son rather than face prison in England. While he was in America his wife died. He then married again, to a young propertied woman, and then left his new wife and young son to fend for themselves while he returned to England. Here he lived in one of the few houses he had managed to keep from his creditors, 6 Carpenter's Place, Walworth Road, and plied his trade as a cabinet maker. It was here that he met Sarah Gale, and had a child by her. Their neighbours thought them married. It was at this juncture that he had met Mr Ward of Tottenham Court Road.

The 'guilty' verdict was returned after only a few minutes. Greenacre was condemned to death and hanged at Newgate on 2 May 1837 whilst Sarah Gale, whom he had continuously insisted knew nothing of the murder, was sentenced to penal servitude. He was allowed to write a letter to his children with the cautionary tale that their Uncle Samuel 'had killed your grandmother and shot off your Aunt Mary's hand'.

six

CHERCHEZ LA FEMME

Most murders in the nineteenth century took place in provincial towns – a London murder was special. The London public's preoccupation with murder reached epic proportions. Its lust for the horror and surreal qualities of a murder was unparalleled. Much of this was fuelled by the newspapers of the time. The following murder is a case in point, as the papers sensationalised it from the outset.

★

The tall, thick-set man, with a long nose bent down towards the tip as if to call attention to an angular jaw that projected out, did not turn up to work at the Port of London on Friday, 10 August 1849. His cousin William Flynn, also a customs officer, was worried. Patrick O'Connor, a 50-year-old Irishman, had long been settled in London and had done very well for himself as a customs officer, fence and loan shark. He enjoyed his job and was popular with his colleagues. When he didn't he turn up on Saturday morning, Flynn and two colleagues, William Keating and David Graham, went to his lodgings. His landlady said she hadn't seen him since Thursday, although she had seen his friend, Mrs Manning, since. Mrs Manning had come, alone, on Thursday and Friday.

The last time Graham and Keating had seen him was on Thursday at a quarter to five in the evening on London Bridge, where O'Connor had shown them a note from Mrs Manning asking him to come to her house at 3 Minver Place, Bermondsey, for supper to meet her lodger's sister.

Who was this Mrs Manning? She was Swiss by birth, originally a lady's maid, aged about 30. She and O'Connor had met in 1842. The much older and well-off Irishman had worked his charms and they had been an item for several years. She had hinted at marriage but he was not interested.

Patrick O'Connor.

Marie Manning.

Minver Place.

She had grown tired of waiting and eventually met a train guard, Frederick Manning. The plump-faced, chinless and malleable Manning had told her he was coming into some money and, spurred on by this, the well-turned-out Marie de Roux accepted his offer of marriage in 1847. It was a mistake. She had only married him to irk O'Connor. She was also a spendthrift, spending money as quickly as Manning earned it. They moved from London to Taunton and back again, taking on the lease of a pub with backing from O'Connor, but nothing seemed to work. She had once left Manning to go back to O'Connor but Manning wooed her back. O'Connor suggested that if they took on a house in Minver Place, Bermondsey, he could rent a room off them. They took the lease of the house, fully expecting him to fulfil his end of the bargain, but he reneged on the deal. He did visit quite often, though, but was becoming tired of Marie and her morose husband. She was irksome baggage as far as O'Connor was concerned, and he now had little to do with her.

The three men went to Arbour Square police station to report O'Connor missing. PC Barnes met Flynn that afternoon and walked to Minver Place to find it locked. Graham and Keating returned to Minver Place on Sunday, only to find Mrs Manning outside her house. She said that O'Connor had never turned up and she had gone to his lodgings to check on him, but he wasn't there either – then again he could be very fickle! Meanwhile Flynn circulated handbills offering a £10 reward over the weekend, to no avail.

On Monday 13 August the police checked the missing man's apartment. His share certificates and money were missing. The next day Meade, a friend of O'Connor's, told Flynn that Mrs Manning had gone. In the evening, PC Burton, Meade and some friends searched 3 Minver Place – to find that all the furniture had gone.

On Friday 17 August, PCs Burton and Barnes made a last search of Minver Place to see if they had missed anything. This time they checked the basement kitchen, which, unlike the rest of the house, was spotless. They noticed that one of the flagstones seemed to have new, wet mortar around it and on an impulse they lifted it with a borrowed crowbar and dug the soft earth underneath it. There, 2ft below, was the naked body of a man, face down, tied up and coated with quicklime. Samuel Lockwood, a surgeon, arrived with a reporter. He felt extensive fractures on the upper part of the skull and pulled out a set of dentures. O'Connor wore dentures. They had found their man.

A further examination, undertaken by the police surgeon George Odling, revealed another fracture extending from the back of the head to the right side and a bullet slug just above the right eye.

The Times of Saturday 18 August headlined 'Extraordinary Discovery of a Murder' and the 'Bermondsey Horror'. Marie Manning was described as a 'native of Geneva, 30 years old, 5ft 7 ins, stout, fresh complexion, with long dark hair, good looking, a scar on the right-hand side of the chin, dresses very smartly, speaks broken English and has been a lady's maid and dressmaker'. *The Times* also stated that 'there can be no doubt that Manning or his wife committed the crime, as they sold all their goods to a broker in Bermondsey Street on Tuesday last, and exhibited a great desire to leave the neighbourhood.'

The findings galvanised the police. Telegraphs were sent to all police stations and ports. Frederick Manning's police description was not flattering: 'Frederick G. Manning, 35 years old, 5ft 8 or 9 ins, stout, very fair and florid complexion, full bloated face, light hair, small sandy whiskers'. An unfortunate couple of the same name boarding a ship bound for New York were arrested and released. Detective Sergeant Shaw established that a Hackney cab driver had picked up Mrs Manning on 13 August near Weston Street: 'a lady of very respectable exterior' with three large boxes, two of which she left, tagged with 'Mrs Smith, passenger to Paris, to be called for', at Waterloo. She then asked to be driven to Euston Station.

Mrs Manning, despite her somewhat superior intelligence, was easy to find. Her clothes and her accent led to her capture. On 21 August Inspector John Haynes of Scotland Yard arrived at Waterloo Station, inspected the boxes left by Mrs Manning and found some of O'Connor's belongings as well as his will dated 6 June 1848, leaving all to Marie. Haynes then went to Euston to discover that a woman answering Marie's description, called Smith, had left Euston on the morning train to Edinburgh on Tuesday 14 August. He sent a telegraph to the Superintendent of the Edinburgh Police.

Marie arrived in Edinburgh on 15 August, booked into a lodging house in Haddington Place under the name of Smith and called in at a draper in Lawnmarket. According to the shop owner, a 'woman of a somewhat elegant appearance speaking with a foreign accent' asked to look at some material and, in passing, queried about a good stockbroker. Armed with the required information, Mrs Smith presented herself at Messrs Hughson and Dobson, members of the Edinburgh Stock Exchange, on Saturday. She asked if they could sell some railway certificates she had and possibly invest £400. They could. She left a £1 scrip certificate with them only to pick it up on Monday, saying that she needed to visit her ailing father before continuing.

On Tuesday 21 August the brokers received notification of the stolen railway certificates and contacted the Edinburgh Police about their suspicions over the Frenchwoman with the Scots father wanting to sell certificates. The police, accompanied by Mr Dobson, first visited the station then the lodging house, where Mr Dobson identified Mrs Smith. She had all the missing certificates, including £115 and seventy-three gold sovereigns! She was, according to the *Edinburgh Courant*, 'attired in an elegant black satin dress and white crepe bonnet … we understand that her manner and accomplishments are most lady-like, and that she talks French with great fluency.'

The perfectly composed Mrs Manning was brought back down to London, taken to Southwark police station and charged with murder. *The Times* described her as wearing:

> a white straw bonnet with a white lace veil … she also wore a black silk mantle with satin stripes with a gown of the same colour and fabric. She is rather above middle height and her figure is stout, without being clumsy. It would, however, be a mistake to call her either handsome or beautiful.

The *Observer*, a leading paper of conjecture and rumour, told its readers that the crime was long premeditated and that the intimacy between O'Connor and Mrs Manning was to be reviled. It portrayed Mrs Manning as both glamorous and repulsive: 'an extremely fine woman, handsome and of almost masculine stature. Her manners at least to the society in which she latterly mixed, appeared those of an accomplished lady.' The *Observer* also went on to report, quite erroneously, that she was a cousin of the Swiss valet François Courvoisier, hanged for the murder of his master, Lord William Russell, in 1840.

But what of Frederick Manning? He, despite being portrayed as less intelligent than his wife, had disappeared completely. An Inspector Perkins had located a cab driver who recalled taking a man fitting Manning's description, along with two bags, from Bermondsey Square to Waterloo Station on 15 August. Many false trails led nowhere. That is until a message reported that a woman had recognised Manning on a Channel steamship heading for Jersey.

He had indeed gone to Jersey, making a nuisance of himself on the boat and in the different hostelries he occupied on the island. He was obnoxiously drunk most of the time and told people how wealthy he was. The Jersey Police were advised he might be there and a Sergeant Langley of Scotland Yard was sent to Jersey.

Manning was arrested on 21 August and returned to London, where he was placed in Horsemonger Lane Gaol along with his wife. He told the police that Marie followed O'Connor to the kitchen, hugged him and calmly shot him and that 'I never liked him so I battered his head with a ripping chisel'.

The inquest of 18 August had established several conclusive facts. William Massey, a medical student who had lodged at the Mannings' house and left a month before the murder, had been introduced to O'Connor several times. Manning had told him that he didn't like O'Connor, and he had also been quizzed by Manning about stupefying drugs. An agent on The Cut established that Manning had purchased a brace of pistols. Manning had also bought a shovel. The Coroner also asked to what extent Mrs Manning could, as a wife, be charged as an active participant in the crime?

The *Observer* of 2 September had offered some guidance to the jury: '…its efforts must have a direct tendency to promote the ends of justice, by setting opinion on the right track I regard to the case at issue.' The jury returned a verdict of murder by both Mannings.

The trial opened on 25 October 1849 before Chief Baron Pollock and Mr Justice Cresswell, the Attorney General. The papers waxed lyrical on the couple:

> No one could help being struck by the contrast between the stamina and impassivity of Marie – who stood motionless and bolt upright in the dock – with the apparent weakness of her husband, who looked ill and had been allowed to remain seated for two days.

Another report described her with a 'thick black veil over the bonnet concealing her features, though when she looked up she bore up with amazing coolness … her eye was bloodshot … and she bore marks of bodily fatigue or mental suffering.' Other reports said that 'Frederick Manning seemed to be some years older than the thirty years'.

The trial was treated like a gala premiere. Admission was by ticket. Count Colloredo, the Austrian Ambassador, his secretary Baron Koller, Prince Richard Metternich and Charles Dickens were among the celebrities who attended. Mrs Manning was determined to fight. She maintained that her husband was the instigator; he had killed through jealousy. The jury retired for three quarters of an hour and returned with a guilty verdict on both of them. Marie then made an appeal based on an ancient statute that a foreigner was entitled to a jury of six Englishmen and six foreigners. This was rejected because she had become a fully-fledged Englishwoman upon marrying Manning.

The *Observer* said that this was the 'most remarkable trial of the century – they both had joint charge of murder.' The *Morning Post* concluded that it had always been premeditated, whilst *The Times* said that the 'announcement was a foregone conclusion'. The *Morning Chronicle* accused Marie of being 'a Lucrecia Borgia or Marquise de Brinvilliers'. The *Manchester Guardian*,

Right: Chief Baron Pollock.
Below: The Mannings and their solicitors.

however, made the most telling comment: '...there is a considerable possibility that judging from the determined and obdurate character of the female, the murder had been planned and to some extent perpetrated by Mrs Manning'.

The couple were hanged on the roof of the gatehouse of Horsemonger Lane Gaol on Tuesday, 13 November 1849. A huge crowd of about 50,000 assembled the night before, Charles Dickens among them. He paid £10 for a rooftop view. Manning admitted his guilt in the end but Marie refused. William Calcraft was the hangman, which was unfortunate as he preferred the short drop. The short drop did not kill the prisoner outright – it could take quite a while for the incumbent to die, up to twenty minutes. Marie's end was magnificent according to one viewer – she was impeccably dressed, while Manning was 'as filthy as a shapeless scarecrow'. Even their end was a show! Marie Manning was the last woman to be hanged in public in England.

Legend has it that the term 'Black Maria', the transport used for felons, originated from the 'black weeds' worn by Mrs Manning. A more tangible origin, however, suggests that the first usage stems from the *Boston Evening Traveler* from 1847, which mentions them as a new type of wagon. *Brewer's Dictionary* suggests the name came from Maria Lee, a large and fearsome black keeper of a sailors' boarding house, who the police would call on for help with difficult prisoners.

The Mannings'
execution at
Horsemonger Lane.

seven

BECAUSE YOU'RE WORTH IT

London, the hub of the greatest empire, attracted the world. Both great and small visited. To some it was the largest and dirtiest city in the world, to others it was the spur for greater riches … and to one in particular it was rich pickings for a lifestyle he had become accustomed to. London was also the setting for one of the most audacious robberies ever perpetrated.

She was beautiful, beguiling and men flocked to see her painting as they had done in her lifetime. Georgiana, Duchess of Devonshire (1757-1806), had been an icon of her time. Born into wealth and married to the older Duke of Devonshire, Georgiana had captured the imagination of an age where a bright, intelligent, and glamorous woman could, and indeed, in her case did, make her mark.

Lionised by society, the bohemian Duchess abided by her rules – to have fun! This

accomplished woman (a linguist amongst her other accomplishments) was considered the most flamboyant, the most shameless and wickedest woman in this *Siècle des Lumières*. She had a *ménage à trois* between her husband and his mistress, had a child by another man, and gambled heavily. She was a society hostess whose parties were legendary. She would also start the fashion for wigs high-topped with feathers and was the first woman to campaign for a candidate in an election in 1784. Her one and only novel, *The Sylph*, is still considered good!

It isn't known exactly when Thomas Gainsborough painted her, but it was possibly in the late 1780s. Gainsborough, though, tried to capture that air of mischief and sensuality that she was known for, and capture it he did – she seductively poses

Georgiana, Duchess of Devonshire.

in the hat she made fashionable, with come-hither eyes. He presented it to the Spencers (Georgiana's family) and when she died in 1806 she and the painting faded from memory until it was rediscovered in 1841 and bought by the dealer, John Bentley, for a derisory sum from a retired schoolteacher.

John Bentley, in turn, sold it on to the MP and collector Wynne Ellis in the 1860s, for £63. Ellis, the most successful silk manufacturer in Britain, also had one of the largest collections of ancient pictures. These he left to the nation on his death in 1875. The trustees of the National Gallery only selected fourteen of the 402 lots, the rest were auctioned off by Christie, Manson & Woods Ltd in five days' sale in May, June and July 1876. *The Times* of 8 May said that '…anyone passing the neighbourhood of St James might well have supposed that some great lady was holding a reception' – and this, in fact, was pretty much what was going on in the Gallery in King Street in the sale of 6 May. Thomas Agnew & Sons, fine art dealers of 39B Bond Street, put in the highest bid for Thomas Gainsborough's portrait of Georgiana, Duchess of Devonshire, at £10,605! It was a great coup and the Agnews were justifiably proud of their acquisition!

The portrait, the most expensive ever purchased, was widely advertised and people came from far and wide to see it. Large posters framed the windows of their premises in Bond Street, heralding their acquisition and the possibility of viewing it, at a price!

Among the paying public streaming to Agnew's Bond Street premises was a well-dressed, mustachioed man-about-town and his personal valet, a beast of a man. They joined the line that wended its way from the ground floor to the first floor, where the lady held court, flanked by the soft glow of two gas lights.

The gentleman's eyes glazed then melted as he too fell under her spell.

On Saturday, 27 May 1876, *The Times*' report on the painting shocked the world:

The picture sold for 10,000 guineas, the highest price ever paid for a portrait, has now been rendered even more so by having been stolen from the gallery in which it had only recently been placed for exhibition, known as the New British Institution, No. 89b Old Bond Street. The greatest excitement arose in the neighbourhood when it became known yesterday morning, soon after 7 o'clock, that this extraordinary and daring robbery had been committed … This room is not 10ft square, having only one window opening on to Bond Street, the other being blocked and covered … The one window was found opened about two feet, and on examining the lead outside there was a distinctly visible mark of a nailed shoe … all the doors were found fastened as they had been left.

It had been expertly cut from the frame, rolled up and passed through the window. Faint traces of grease on the floor, approximately the size of the painting, showed that the thief knew what he had been doing – he had spread a thin veneer of it on the canvas so as to keep it supple!

It had been an easily executed robbery. At least three men had been involved; one to act as lookout, another for a hoist up for the third, who jemmied the first floor window open, slid into the room and prised the canvas off the frame, passing it back down to his comrade below.

No amount of searching or questioning informants answered any questions. The mystery of the stolen Duchess would not be resolved until the end of the century. Scotland Yard, though, had their suspicions – Pinkerton Detective Agency had contacted them about the notorious thief Adam Worth, who, under the pseudonym Henry Judson Raymond, an affluent American, had come to England in 1875.

Thirty-five-year-old Henry J. Raymond arrived in London in 1875, fresh from a very successful venture in Paris, renting a spacious West End flat at 198 Piccadilly (now 198-202) and leasing the more spacious Western Lodge on Clapham Common, complete with coach house and large garden. Here he would entertain the great and the good.

It was at Western Lodge, exquisitely furnished with the finest antique furniture and paintings, where Henry J. Raymond, his mistress Kitty Flynn, and his close associate 'Piano' Charley Bullard, lived. It was also where, reputedly, a rolled up canvas of the 'Lady' remained hidden in the coach house for nearly a decade.

The grand house, with views on the Common, had its own specially appointed guards – Her Majesty's police constables – patrolling its outer perimeter. They were there to keep a watch on Henry J. Raymond, but to no avail.

This quiet American kept a string of horses and a yacht, and had a reputed income of at least £30,000 per annum – he certainly spent £20,000 a year! He was also the most successful criminal of the nineteenth century, quite possibly of all time.

Adam Worth was not the debonair master criminal so loved of the classic detective genre, nor was he a cruel and evil-looking arch criminal. He was a cut above both. He did not drink, he did not fight, nor did he resort to violence. He made his career – for career it was – a profession, and chose his colleagues with care. He had fled the parental home at about the age of 10, moved to New York and was a protégé of the celebrated Marm Mandelbaum, from whom he learnt the art of delegating and organising gangs.

Western Lodge, Clapham.

He joined the Union army in the Civil War and made a tidy sum joining regiments under assumed names, being paid, and then deserting. It was then that Pinkerton's started taking an active interest in him. He certainly spent some time behind bars but always managed to escape. His forte was forgery and supreme organisational skills. He established, in all the cities he made home, gangs of thieves who had no idea who the organiser behind their thefts was. He was a true 'Napoleon of Crime', whose very name prompted complete devotion from his followers, and fear in the police. His 'work' certainly influenced many detective writers; Conan-Doyle's Professor Moriarty is certainly based on him, and perhaps Maurice Leblanc's Arsène Lupin.

Detective Inspector John Shore of Scotland Yard made it his life's work to bring Worth to justice – with no effect. Worth had little or no time for the London Police. He found them disorganised.

Adam Worth, aka Henry J. Raymond.

The painting, a hot property, could not be sold – or would not be sold by its new owner. Worth decided that a break from London was needed. He went to South Africa to make some more money. His fortunes, however, declined. He also spent some seven years in a Belgian prison. Whilst in prison he was beaten up by confederates of an ex-partner in crime and returned to lick his wounds in America.

It wasn't until 1897 when a dispirited Adam Worth approached William Pinkerton. He and Pinkerton had a high regard for each other's professionalism. This turned into a friendship that was to last until Worth's death. Worth agreed that he would sell the painting, with Pinkerton acting as intermediary, on condition that Worth was not prosecuted. The painting was sold for $25,000 in 1901. It was eventually resold to the Duke of Devonshire in 1992. Worth returned to England to be with his family, dying in 1902, and is buried in Highgate Cemetery.

eight

JACK THE RIPPER

London, in the last quarter of the nineteenth century, was the largest and richest city in the world. The attractions of the West End contrasted starkly with those of the East End.

The East End, specifically Whitechapel, had been fields in the seventeenth century. By the end of the next century the industrial demands of the Port of London and ancillary industries had created the development of a rash of small buildings and a warren of streets, into which crammed poor immigrant workers living cheek-by-jowl next to the indigenous London poor. Nearly 90 per cent of its inhabitants were immigrants and prejudice was rife. The poorest people lived in grim slums or in common boarding houses.

By 1888 there were just over 200 common boarding houses accommodating 8,500 people. Many of the women living in these relied on prostitution for extra money. There were at least 1,500 prostitutes in Whitechapel alone.

By day Whitechapel was a riot of colour and infernal noise, where everyone struggled to make enough money to feed themselves once a day. By night the public houses, prostitutes and street gangs plied their trade. Life was desperate and often short.

The murders of 1888 that brought national and international notoriety to Whitechapel coincided with the rash of cheap newspapers that were to make it so notorious: it was the year when all taxes on newspapers were finally abolished, enabling these to produce cheaper reading material for a larger section of the newly literate public. The public was now catered for in local, national and international news, not forgetting sensationalism. Newspapers mushroomed all over England. What certain newspapers forgot in the rush to make money, however, was that publishing news brought a certain public responsibility. The brutal killings in Whitechapel demonstrated the power and the irresponsible journalism of many papers.

The East End already had an insalubrious reputation and was known for gratuitous violence and the occasional murder, but the brutal murder of a woman in 1888 heralded a new dawn for the media and the annals of crime.

At 4.45 a.m. on 7 August 1888, the bloodied body of 37-year-old prostitute Martha Tabrams was found on a landing of George Yard Buildings. She was punctured with thirty-nine stab wounds, one of which seemed to have been made by a bayonet. Most of the wounds were around the sex organs, implying that the attack was sexual.

Martha was known to the police and had lived in a common boarding house in George Street. The last time she had been seen alive was when she and a friend, 'Pearly Poll' Connolly, were draped drunkenly over two soldiers outside the White Swan pub in Whitechapel Road at 11 p.m. the previous night.

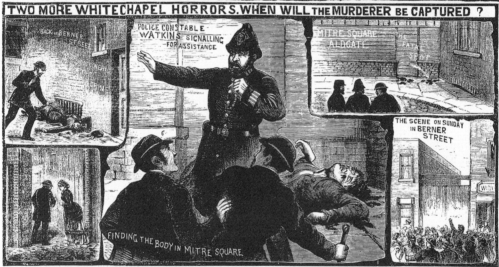

The Whitechapel murders.

The police followed the only clues available, that of the bayonet wound and its military connotation. These led nowhere, as the two soldiers had acceptable alibis and second-hand bayonets could be purchased from most stalls in East End markets. The inquest of 9 August resulted in the open verdict of 'murder by person or persons unknown'. *The Times'* austere reportage differed markedly from the sensationalist articles published by the Sunday and evening papers.

The whispers had barely died down when the next murder in Whitechapel took hold of the public imagination.

Mary Ann 'Polly' Nicholls was a pretty, dark-haired, young-looking 44-year-old woman. She was literate, close to her parents, but her recourse to drinking had broken up an otherwise stable marriage to a printer, William Nicholls.

From 1882 until the summer of 1888, Mary Ann had been in and out of Lambeth Workhouse with the occasional return to her parents. A final stab at a respectable job 'in service' in Wandsworth ended when she absconded with items belonging to her employers in July 1888. She finally ended up, on 24 August, at a boarding house known as 'The White House' at 56 Flower and Dean Street.

It had been a heavy night for Mary Ann on 30 August 1888. She had been seen walking down the Whitechapel Road towards the Frying Pan pub at 11 p.m., eventually pouring out of it past midnight and ending up a little more sober in the kitchen of another boarding house in Thrawl Street at 1.20 a.m.

At 2.30 a.m. her friend, Emily Holland, found her drunk outside a grocer's shop at the corner of Osborne Street, opposite Whitechapel Church. Emily tried to persuade Mary Ann to come home with her, but she refused. It would be the last time Emily saw her friend alive.

Buck's Row (later re-named Durward Street) was a narrow cobbled street with two-storey houses on one side and industrial premises on the other. Charles Cross, a Pickford's driver, was walking to work down the Essex Wharf side of Buck's Row at 3.30 a.m. on 31 August when he saw the body of a woman lying against some stable yard gates. He called over a passer-by and both men grabbed a passing policeman.

The workhouse stamp on the woman's petticoat eventually established her identity – that of Mary Ann Nicholls.

Dr Rees Ralph Llewellyn performed the autopsy at the mortuary in Old Montague Street, with Inspector John Spratling in attendance. She had been butchered. Apart from two very deep cuts in the throat that virtually severed the head from the body, there was a vicious jagged cut running down the left

Buck's Row.

side of her abdomen and several cuts down the right side. The private parts had, like Martha Tabrams', been the primary object of the assault. It was evident that her killer had been left-handed and had anatomical knowledge. The attack would have only taken five minutes.

Inspector Helson, the Senior Inspector, thought that Mary Ann had been murdered *in situ*, although the papers surmised that she may have been killed somewhere else and dumped in Buck's Row, and that a gang may have been involved.

The Times of 1 September was quite categorical:

> … viewing the spot where the body was found, it seems difficult to believe that the woman received her death wounds there … If the woman was murdered on the spot where the body was found, it is almost impossible to believe that she would not have aroused the neighbourhood with her screams.

The article added that none of the internal organs were missing.

The next day a local firm suggested that a reward might be offered for information. The Home Secretary, Henry Matthews, rejected this idea, to his cost!

What Scotland Yard did decide, however, was that the East End police needed a senior inspector who knew the area well and had some standing in the community. They chose Inspector Frederick Abberline (1843-1930). He was a CID Inspector at Whitehall who had been at Whitechapel from 1873-1887. Well-liked, efficient, and an officer with a promising future, Abberline's avuncular exterior held a razor sharp and analytical mind that would be put to great use in future cases, notably the Cleveland Street Scandal. DC Walter Dew (of later Crippen fame) was one of those who welcomed their inspector back.

Despite Abberline's return, the police made no headway on this murder either. The newspapers described the East End as the 'Heart of Darkness' or a 'Terra Incognita', creating an even greater divide between the genteel West End and the poor East End.

Papers competed with one another to produce theories about the murder. William Le Queux, of *The Globe*, Charles Hands of the *Pall Mall Gazette*, and Lincoln Springfield of *The Star* would take it in turns to publish different theories about how the murders had been committed.

Annie Chapman, better known as Annie Sivvey or Dark Annie, was a friendly 47-year-old brunette who resorted to prostitution when selling matches, antimacassars and flowers couldn't pay the rent or buy food. Her coachman husband, John Chapman, had left her in 1885, taking their two children with him, because of her drinking, although he had continued

Henry Matthews.

Inspector F. Abberline.

PC Walter Dew.

to give her a weekly stipend until his death in 1886. She had then taken up with a Jack Sivvey, amongst other men. The only time she drank was at weekends, and on Saturday 8 September she left her lodgings in Dorset Street, to go down Paternoster Row at 1.35 a.m. She said she was going to make some money to pay for her bed. This was the last time she was definitely seen alive.

Number 29 Hanbury Street was a wooden house housing seventeen people, at the front of which were two doors, one leading into a shop, the other into a passage leading to stairs to the various floors and a door with steps leading down to a yard with a recess to its side, next to a fence separating the property from another.

At 5.15 a.m. the next-door carpenter, Mr Cadosch, went to his yard toilet and heard people talking in the yard next door, followed by a thud against the fence. Shortly after, at 5.30 a.m., a woman saw a man whom she took to be a Jew talking to a woman she thought she recognised as Annie Chapman outside 29 Hanbury Street.

At 6 a.m. Police Inspector Chandler of Commercial Street Station received notice of the discovery of a murder some fifteen minutes earlier at 29 Hanbury Street. Dr George Bagster Phillips, the Police Divisional Surgeon, arrived half an hour later.

Annie Chapman's body, legs drawn up and knees splayed outwards, was tucked in the recess of the yard.

The details of this murder were not made public for good reason. It was a particularly gruesome murder. The *Lancet* would publish this later. She had first been strangled, and then her throat slit to drain the body of blood. The body was then mutilated blood-free. The throat was cut to the spine from left to right, indicating a right-handed assailant. The abdomen had been slit open; the severed intestines had been lifted out and placed on the right shoulder. The pelvic area was totally mutilated; the uterus, the upper portion of the vagina and two thirds of the bladder had been entirely removed. The doctor admitted that this mutilation would have taken nearly an hour and the murderer had probably used a small amputating knife with a blade of about 6-9 inches in length. He also thought that the murder may have occurred at about 4.30 a.m., although he suggested that the cold may have made the time of death an hour later. This implied that Mr Cadosch may have heard the murder taking place.

Because of the mutilations, Abberline agreed that Chapman and Nicholls had been murdered by the same person. The killer was obviously unhinged and had medical knowledge. On the strength of this slender clue the police would try to trace three 'insane' medical students – two were traced and one had gone abroad. Another unstable man, a failed barrister, Montague John Druitt, was also sought by the police.

The Press, in the dark about the mutilations, surmised. The pure sensationalism of *The Star* gave it 261,000 sales per day! *The Times* would surmise on 9 September that the murderer was not a member of the working classes and was possibly a lodger.

On 25 September the Central News Agency received a letter signed 'Jack The Ripper'. This would, unfortunately, start the legend and spawn an industry. The police would later admit that it was a hoax made by an 'enterprising' journalist.

A greater police presence did not guarantee a safer neighbourhood. Israel Schwartz, a Hungarian Jew, had just reached the gateway of the yard of the International Workers' Educational Club on Berner Street at 00.45 a.m. on Sunday 30 September when he saw a man with dark hair and small brown moustache speak to a woman at the gateway. They scuffled and he pushed her into the street before throwing her onto the footway. Not wanting to be involved, Schwartz crossed the street, noticing a man with a pipe in the doorway of another house. He couldn't see the man properly but he did recognise the woman. She was a local prostitute, Lizzie Stride, and it was the last time she was seen alive.

Berner Street.

The International Workers' Educational Club had been founded by a group of Jewish Socialists in 1884. It was a hive of radical thought, provided food and lodging as well as entertainment for the radical political elite of the East End. Its largely immigrant patrons were considered evil and depraved by the native Eastenders. This led to more friction and fights than normal.

Louis Diemschutz, the Steward of the Club and a travelling jewellery salesman, was just returning from Norwood in a pony and trap at one o'clock when his horse shied away from a corner of the Club yard. He noticed a bundle on the ground and saw it was the body of a woman. He rushed to tell the Club members and then went off to find a policeman. Two policemen were found, one of whom fetched Dr Blackwell of Commercial Road. Dr Phillips, the police surgeon, arrived at 1.25 a.m. Lizzie Stride was easily identified.

Fourty-four-year-old Lizzie Stride had started early, as a prostitute, in her native Sweden. One of the many immigrants to the East End, she was known to the Swedish authorities, had married several times, and had recently been lodging at 32 Flower and Dean Street. Her current boyfriend, Michael Kidney, had seen her for the last time on 25 September. She was a quiet, conscientious woman with a sense of humour when she had work. Many thought they had seen her at various times that night but most sightings were discarded as invention or embellishment.

She was found lying on her back close to the wall by the gates of the Club. Her extended left hand held a packet of lozenges. Her right arm, the hand and wrist covered with blood, was over her belly – she had obviously tried to staunch the blood with it. The legs were drawn up and both shoulders had a bluish discolouration, implying that two hands had pressed down on the shoulders. The throat had been cut from left to right, severing the carotid artery – her assailant had attacked her from behind, ensuring no blood on his clothes. There were no other wounds. Was the killer interrupted? Phillips agreed that the murderer knew where to cut. But was it the 'Ripper'?

Not forty-five minutes later, PC Watkin, on a return journey to Mitre Square, found the body of a middle-aged woman in a dark corner of the Square. He called a night watchman to fetch another policeman. PCs Harvey and Holland arrived, Holland being despatched to call for a surgeon. Doctors George Sequeira and Frederick Gordon Brown arrived within ten minutes. Only an hour later PC Alfred Long was passing 118-119 Goulston Buildings when he noticed a torn, bloodied piece of apron that matched the one worn by the victim, and on the wall a chalk-written message: 'The Jewes are the men that will not be blamed for nothing.' It is a shame that a photographer never took a picture and that the sign was erased on the orders of Sir Charles Warren, the Police Commissioner.

Sir Charles Warren.

The Press widely asserted that the killer could have been a Jew. Even Matthews, the Home Secretary, came to the conclusion that the killer was a Jew – after all, an Englishman could never bow to such morbid proclivities …

The second victim of the night was well known to the police. Catherine Eddowes (aka Kate Kelly) had just been released from Bishopsgate police station at the time Stride's body had been discovered. She had been drunk a few hours before and placed in a cell to sober up. She was last seen walking towards Houndsditch.

Catherine was 45, had had children but had fallen out with her family because of her drinking habit and migrated to London. She lodged at 55 Flower and Dean Street, earning a crust from prostitution, hop-picking and scrounging off her daughter. Her current partner, John Kelly, had last seen her at about 11 p.m. the previous evening. Apart from the police, a Joseph Lawende had possibly been the last person to see her, at 1.35 a.m., at the corner of Church Passage and Duke Street. She was talking to a man whose description seemed to fit with that of Schwartz's description of the man seen with Lizzie Stride.

This time the police kept quiet. The Press complained that they were receiving no new information and that Mr Lawende was being separated from the public.

The injuries were horrific: Dr Gordon Brown noted that the face was severely cut. The eyes, nose, lips and cheeks were severely hacked. The throat had been cut and the abdomen had been the primary target – the left kidney and uterus were missing. Doctors Brown and Sequeira agreed that the killer did not have a great anatomical skill. This was also Dr W.S. Saunders' opinion. The killer possessed a good deal of knowledge as to the position of the organs and how to remove them, but this could have been done by someone used to cutting up animals. Dr Phillips concurred with their findings.

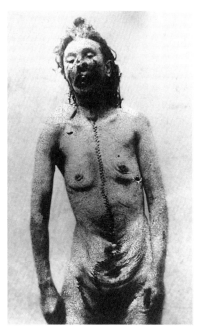

The mutilated corpse of Catherine Eddowes.

The Home Secretary was publicly castigated for not offering a reward. He now wrote to Sir Charles Warren saying that he would, on the condition that Warren publicly admitted the incompetence of the police.

One curious anomaly was that Israel Schwartz, who had last seen the first of that night's victims, did not appear at the inquest nor was his account known until the Home Office files were opened to public inspection. His evidence, however, had been considered of sufficient interest and importance to the police to keep it from the public and refer to it several times. It was only reported on 10 October in *The Star*.

The tall, pretty, blonde and educated Mary Jane Kelly was behind with her rent on the night of Friday 9 November. The manager of her lodging house at Miller's Court asked his deputy to ask her for some rent at 10.45 p.m. He tried her door, but it was locked. He pushed back the curtains from a broken window to find her two severed breasts on a table. By 11.30 p.m. Inspector Abberline and Dr Phillips had arrived. Photographs were taken and the locked door was forced.

Dr Thomas Bond, who conducted the post-mortem, concluded that the attacker had no scientific knowledge. She was asleep and in her bedclothes at the time of the attack. The whole of the abdomen had been opened and emptied of its contents. The face was hacked beyond recognition and the neck tissues were severed to the bone. The uterus and kidneys were under her head.

Aside from a severed kidney received by post, and ultimately rejected as evidence, the brutal murders stopped after Kelly. The police agreed that at least five of the murders were committed by the same person. Sir Charles Warren resigned. Abberline remained convinced that the killer was one George Chapman, a barber surgeon, despite no tangible evidence. He would later say, 'theories, we were lost almost in theories; there were so many of them.' The hapless barrister Montague John Druitt committed suicide in November, leading many to think that he might have been the killer.

Fleet Street had done its worst damage. It had turned the murders into a media event by stressing the inherently dangerous nature of the East End. The 'Ripper' murders prompted the papers to promote a moral and social panic that swept through the City and beyond. The *Daily Chronicle* of 10 September was to encapsulate the public's alarm by calling Whitechapel 'The Eastern Murderland'. The *Evening News* of the same date stressed the sex element, with 'the murders' being 'erotomanic' and showing 'amatory desires of an inordinate nature'. Other papers stayed aloof, maintaining a conciliatory moral tone, such as the *Bath and Cheltenham Gazette*, who maintained that 'the excitement has largely been stimulated and fed by the unnecessary prominence given to the subject and by the many foolish rumours which have been published.'

The Ripper myth continues to occupy our minds because of its huge initial media coverage and the lack of any tangible clues. It is, most probably, the most famous unsolved case in the world because of the papers. Rumour and gossip have created an industry that just won't go away. More than a hundred books and pamphlets have been written about the subject with a list of suspects that range from the sublime to the ridiculous. Prince Albert Victor, grandson of Queen Victoria and most probably involved in the 'Cleveland Street Scandal', was one; Dr William Gull, Physician to the Queen, another. A range of Jewish Eastenders also feature amongst the suspects, showing that prejudice was, and remains, rife. Foreigners also feature largely amongst these, such as Dr Thomas Neill Cream (*see* chapter ten), Walter Sickert, the artist, and Dr Alexander Pedachenko, a mad Russian secret agent. There will, undoubtedly, be others . . .

'Who was Jack The Ripper?'

nine

'THE ABOMINABLE CRIME OF BUGGERY'

During a routine investigation of petty pilfering amongst the messenger boys at the Central Post Office, St Martin's Le Grand, PC Luke Hanks questioned 15-year-old Charles Swinscomb on Thursday, 4 July 1889.

Swinscomb had an unusual amount of money on him. He maintained that he had received this for private work. What private work? From Mr Charles Hammond at 19 Cleveland Street, 'for going to bed with a gentleman'! He had been asked by a clerk, Henry Newlove, if he had wanted to earn some extra money and he had been there twice. Swinscomb had also mentioned that Newlove had persuaded two other boys to do the same: George Alma Wright and Charles Ernest Thickbroom. All three were suspended from work hours later and PC Hanks went to his superiors with the appalling news of the discovery of a male brothel.

Homosexuality was known to exist but was conveniently brushed under the carpet by Victorian Society. Homosexuality among men was a crime punishable by imprisonment. Henry Labouchère successfully amended the homosexuality laws to make any homosexual act between men a crime in 1885. Curiously, however, homosexuality in women was 'officially' non-existent.

Police Commissioner James Monro assigned his best detective inspector to the case the following day – DI George Abberline. Abberline, veteran of the Whitechapel murders

Charles Hammond.

The three telegraph boys.

49

and possibly the most high-profile detective at Scotland Yard, acted quickly and had a warrant to arrest Henry Newlove and Charles Hammond on the grounds 'that they did unlawfully, wickedly and corruptly conspire, combine and confederate and agree to incite and procure George Alma Wright and divers other persons to commit the abominable crime of buggery' on 6 July. By the time they reached the scene of the crime, Charles Hammond had gone. He'd been warned by Newlove and had fled.

Meanwhile, PC Hanks went to arrest Newlove at his family home in Camden on Sunday 7 July. On their journey to the station, Newlove moaned that he thought it 'very hard that I should get into trouble while men in high position are allowed to walk about free … Lord Arthur Somerset, the Earl of Euston and Colonel Jervois go regularly there.' Newlove would repeat this to Abberline the next day. This put a completely new angle on this case.

Hanks re-visited Newlove's home only to overhear a visitor, 'Reverend' George Veck, talk about looking after Henry Newlove and Mr Hammond. The name rang a bell; he recalled an incident in Gravesend when a telegraphist called Veck was sacked for homosexuality. Subsequently Abberline put a watch on 19 Cleveland Street. The officer on watch reported seeing an MP and Lord Arthur Somerset visiting. Swinscomb and Thickbroom both identified Somerset a week later.

Abberline's suspicions on the seriousness of the case were further confirmed when Veck produced Arthur Newton, a young solicitor known for taking on embarrassing cases. It was only on 8 August that the Director of Public Prosecutions started proceedings against Veck, Lord Arthur Somerset and Hammond. Until then various government departments had refused to take the responsibility and, curiously enough, even the Prime Minister, Lord Salisbury, was taking an interest, specifically refusing permission for the police to pursue Hammond to France.

The police finally caught up with Veck on 20 August at Waterloo Station, with some very incriminating letters in his pockets. These were from one Algernon Allies, who said

Left to right: Detective Inspector Frederick Abberline, Lord Arthur Somerset, The Earl of Euston.

that a 'Mr Brown' gave him money for services rendered. The dogged PC Hank went to interview Allies, who admitted that 'Mr Brown' was Lord Arthur Somerset.

There was a clear case against Somerset. He was, though, a member of the aristocracy, an officer and a member of the Prince of Wales's staff. The responsibility for bringing Somerset to justice was shunted from one department to the next, finally resting with the Director of Public Prosecution, who was asked to treat this with discretion, i.e. no proceedings against Somerset and allowing him leave to flee to France. The powerless Abberline and his superiors were to ask themselves what exactly was it that made government departments, let alone the Prime Minister, hinder the wheels of justice.

On 18 September, Veck and Newlove were brought to trial (Hammond conveniently absent) and indicted on thirteen counts of procuring six boys to 'commit acts of gross indecency with another person'. Lord Salisbury specifically vetoed Hammond's extradition from America as he did 'not consider this to be a case in which any official application could justifiably be made'. Another deal was also made with the two defendants. If they pleaded guilty to indecency, then conspiracy and procuring would not be pressed, enabling Veck to only receive nine months' imprisonment and Newlove four. The Assistant Director of Public Prosecution, Hamilton Cuffe, considered it a 'travesty of justice'. Things could surely not get worse?

Abberline was contacted by Allies on 25 September. Somerset had returned to England and tried to bribe him to leave the country, saying that 'the reason to want you to get away is that you should not give your evidence against you know who'. Who was who? Obviously a very important person. They set a trap for that evening, only to catch Newton's clerk, Taylorson. Newton immediately warned Somerset to leave the country.

Once again the police had been outmanoeuvred. They did advise the Prince of Wales who, disbelieving Somerset's inclinations, had to be convinced by the Prime Minister. Somerset resigned his commission and on 12 September warrants were issued against him for committing acts of gross indecency, procuring Allies to commit similar crimes with other males, and conspiring with Charles Hammond to procure such acts contrary to the Criminal Law Amendment Act 1885. Somerset, however, would never return to England.

The foreign Press weren't hampered with libel laws; Paris papers screamed that dozens of peers were involved and that London was the 'modern Sodom'. The New York papers went further, implicating Prince Albert Victor, the Prince of Wales's son, already a popular suspect in the 'Ripper' case, in the 'Cleveland Street Scandal'. Back home the scandal would erupt magnificently with the 16 September headlines of a radical London paper, *North London Press*, screaming: 'The West End Scandals' and contending that two leading aristocrats, Lord Arthur Somerset and Lord Euston, had left the country because of their proclivities. Its editor, Ernest Parke, and W.T. Stead, editor of the *Pall Mall Gazette*, and Henry Labouchère, all radicals, suspected an official conspiracy.

The riposte was just as fierce. Lord Euston instructed his solicitor to institute proceedings against Parke for libel. Parke retorted with a succinct article setting out his suspicions and confirming that he was the subject of a libel action.

The libel trial was held on 15 January 1890 at the Old Bailey. It was a show trial where the establishment outwitted the rest. Six defence witnesses first gave evidence; five of them were too unsophisticated to be reliable and their evidence was rejected. Euston took the stand last and remained unexamined until all the defence witnesses had given evidence. Only one witness, Jack Saul, a bright and eloquent male prostitute and pimp, gave the

The Cleveland Street Scandal.

exact details of when he met with Euston and Newlove. He had, some months before, made a statement to the police to that effect, but the police were not allowed to follow it up. If Saul's assertions were false why wasn't he prosecuted for perjury? Labouchère was to make this observation in his paper, *Truth*. Nor were the police allowed to bring two of the messenger boys to identify Euston. The judge directed the jury adroitly – would they believe a man of the street or an educated one? Parke was found guilty of libel without justification.

The scandal died with Prince Albert Victor in 1892, but in a letter to Oliver Montagu, a member of the royal entourage, Somerset would say:

I cannot see what good I could do to Prince Eddy [Albert Victor] if I went into court … I might do him harm … I have never mentioned the boy's name except to … Had they been wise, hearing what I knew and therefore what others knew they ought to have hushed the matter up … Nothing will ever make me divulge anything I know even if I were arrested … But if I went into court and told all I knew no one who called himself a man would ever speak to me again.

ten

HAVE SOME MEDICINE M'DEAR

London was the capital of capitals in the late nineteenth century. The whole world came to the city where sin was a pleasure and 'sometimes pleasure's a sin'. Many came to sample the hub of the world's greatest empire. Some arrived having fled political injustices, others came to start over for completely different reasons. Dr Thomas Neill Cream, who booked into Anderton's Hotel, 163 Fleet Street on 5 October 1891, was one of the latter.

The eldest of eight siblings, Cream was born in Glasgow in 1850. The family left for Canada four years later, where the father built up a shipbuilding firm. Thomas became a medical student at McGill University, graduating with merit in 1876. His only obvious shortcoming was a painful squint, which he alleviated with a constant supply of morphine.

The newly qualified Cream proved quite adept at backstreet abortions and swindling insurance companies. He also met, impregnated and subsequently carried out a brutal abortion upon Flora Brooks, the daughter of a wealthy hotelier. The ensuing shotgun marriage made Cream bolt for England, where he enrolled as a postgraduate student at St Thomas's Hospital and rounded off his education with a qualification from the Royal College of Physicians and Surgeons at Edinburgh. He returned to Canada – when his wife died of consumption – to claim $1,000 under the marriage contract. He only got $200.

He resumed his lucrative career of backstreet abortions, only to suffer a setback when the body of a young woman was found in his practice toilet. It was fairly obvious that he had killed her, but lack of direct evidence got him off. He moved to Chicago, continuing with his unsavoury practice and building up a business selling a 'medicine' that cured epilepsy. The pretty young wife of an impressed client was sent to him. She fell under his spell, whilst her husband died of a mysterious ailment. Cream's predilection for sending fantasy letters would prove to be his undoing in this case, and fatal in the future. In Chicago he sent fantasy letters to the District Attorney, saying that it had been the chemist's fault for putting too much strychnine in the husband's medicine. Cream was sent to jail for life.

Cream's father died in 1887. His family pressed for an early release, and, allowing for good behaviour, he was released on 31 July 1891, collecting a $16,000 inheritance and leaving for Britain.

The tall, balding gentleman with cross-eyes, bushy moustache and silk hat hit the town on Tuesday 6 October. 'Fred' picked up a prostitute, Elizabeth Masters, in Ludgate Circus, went home with her to Hercules Road, off Lambeth Road, and then disported himself at Gatti's Emporium on Westminster Bridge Road.

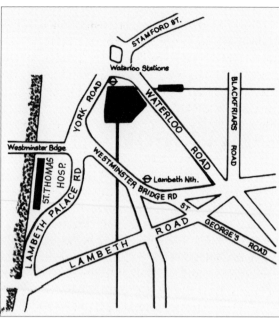

Dr Neil Cream.   Map of the Waterloo area.

Despite the redevelopment of this part of Lambeth following the creation of yet another railway station, Waterloo, the area was known as one of the seediest and dirtiest parts of London, where light industries servicing the station mixed with the oldest profession in the world. This was one of the largest red light districts, where young women plied their trade from dingy backstreets. It was also where the disturbed Cream took up residence at 103 Lambeth Palace Road on Wednesday 7 October.

On 9 October, the attractive 27-year-old Matilda Clover, mother of a 2-year-old boy, met a man called 'Fred' whom she took home to 27 Lambeth Road. 'Fred' had made an appointment with Miss Masters, but saw Matilda and made a beeline for her. Masters and a friend saw them and followed.

The following day Dr Cream purchased a quantity of Nux Vomica, containing strychnine, and a box of gelatine capsules from Mr Priest's chemist shop at 22 Parliament Street.

A 19-year-old prostitute, Ellen Donworth, collapsed in convulsions on Waterloo Road on the evening of 13 October 1891. A patron of the Wellington pub, on the other side of the street, helped her up and took her home to 8 Duke (Duchy) Street, where, in a lull in her dramatic convulsions, she explained to her landlady and Inspector Harvey of the Lambeth division, a previous client, that Fred, 'a tall gentleman with cross eyes, a silk hat and bushy whiskers', had given her a drink with white stuff in it. Mr Johnson, of the South London Medical Institute, diagnosed that her convulsions were similar to those caused by an overdose of strychnine. She was rushed to St Thomas's Hospital, where she died in agony. Her post-mortem revealed a quarter of a grain of strychnine in her stomach.

The Deputy Coroner, Mr George Wyatt, received a strange letter demanding £300,000 in exchange for information on the murder of Miss Donworth. He filed it for future reference and the inquest gave a verdict of 'death by poisoning with strychnine and morphia by a person unknown'.

One of Matilda Clover's housemates saw a letter Matilda received asking to meet the writer, Fred, on 20 October. She was to bring the letter with her. Matilda brought the tall, mustachioed, heavily-built man back to her lodgings. He left late. At about three in the morning the house was woken up by screams of agony. Matilda was writhing on her bed. She said that Fred had given her some pills. Her alcoholism made Dr McCarthy's assistant, Mr Coppin, think that her fits were due to chronic alcoholism. She died in agony and the following day her doctor, Dr Graham, ascribed her death to alcohol poisoning. Matilda was buried in Tooting Cemetery on 27 October.

A flurry of rather extraordinary letters was received by divers individuals. These letters were to cast doubt on the 'natural' death of Miss Clover. Countess Russell received a letter accusing her husband of poisoning Clover: a Mr Malone sent a letter to the eminent Dr William Broadbent, threatening to expose him as the murderer of Miss Emma Clover unless he paid £2,500, and finally Messrs W.H. Smith & Sons received a letter accusing Mr F.W.D. Smith of murdering Ellen Donworth.

London was quiet for the next few months – because Cream had fallen in love, proposed and been accepted by a Miss Sabatini of Berkhamsted. He then returned to Canada, where he had printed 500 copies of another totally unbelievable fantasy letter addressed to the guests of the Metropole Hotel. He returned to his London lodgings in early April 1902.

PC George Cumley was walking his beat at 2.15 a.m. on 12 April. As he passed down Stamford Street he noticed that a young woman was seeing a large, bespectacled, mustachioed man in a tall silk hat and cape out of No. 118. The man disappeared towards Waterloo Road. His return beat brought him back to the same address forty-five minutes later.

Matilda Clover.

Ellen Donworth's Death

To the Guests,

Of the Metropole Hotel.

Ladies and Gentlemen,

I hereby notify you that the person who poisoned Ellen Donworth

On the 13th last October is today in the employ of the Metropole Hotel

And that your lives are in danger as long as you remain in this hotel.

Yours respectfully,

W.H. MURRAY

London April   1892

Accusatory letter addressed to the Metropole Hotel.

A cab stood outside, as did a PC Eversfield, with a bundle in his arms. It was the girl Cumley had seen earlier, Emma Shrivell, an 18-year-old prostitute. Both Shrivel and her 21-year-old friend, Alice Marsh, had woken the house up with their screams and their landlord had called Eversfield. Alice Marsh died on the way to St Thomas's Hospital; Shrivell died six hours later. The police began to suspect that a serial murderer was at work. They eventually had Matilda Clover's body exhumed.

On 26 April, Dr Joseph Harper of Barnstaple received a letter from a W.H. Murray, claiming that his son, a medical student at St Thomas's and lodger at 103 Lambeth Palace Road, was the murderer of the two girls of Stamford Street. The information could be suppressed with the payment of £1,500. Dr Harper thought the writer a madman and ignored this ludicrous threat. He was, indeed, quite right. At least so thought Miss Sleaper, landlady of both Cream and Harper Junior, when she heard this from Cream's own lips!

Further letters were sent to the Coroner, Mr Wyatt, and to Mr George Clarke, a detective of Cockspur Street. Meanwhile John Haynes, erstwhile engineer and part-time secret agent, lodger of Mr and Mrs Armstead of 129 Westminster Road, was introduced to a balding, large myopic man, a friend of his landlord, a certain Dr Neill of Canada. As both men had been to America they seemed to have much in common. Eventually Cream began to boast about his familiarity with the murders and even took Haynes on a guided tour of the murder spots! Haynes often crossed Westminster Bridge to see his friend, Police Sergeant McIntyre of Scotland Yard, and talked to him, among other things, about this rather eccentric character, Dr Neill.

This possible lead intrigued McIntyre. He set a watch on the doctor's perambulations. Quite by chance, Constable Cumley recognised Dr Cream as he started to follow a prostitute down St George's Road, then into a house on Elliott's Row. He waited and followed Cream back to his lodgings. After this, Cream became paranoid that he was being tailed and told his friend Haynes, who in turn questioned McIntyre – McIntyre remained non-committal. Cream however pursued it, accosting McIntyre as he was leaving Haynes's lodgings. Intrigued, McIntyre decided to look into this and discovered PC Cumley's statement about the man seen leaving 118 Stamford Street. It was just too convenient for comfort.

McIntyre visited Cream at his lodgings and requested a list of his movements while he was in England. Cream, in a panic, wrote a letter of complaint, via his solicitors, to the Chief Commissioner of Police, Sir Edward Bradford. Inspector Tunbridge was instructed to look into the South Lambeth poisoning cases. He visited Cream and was shown a medical case containing, among other bottles, a bottle of strychnine grains. Tunbridge also visited Dr Harper and realised that the blackmail letter was in Cream's handwriting. They could nail him for blackmail!

On 3 June, protesting his innocence, Cream was arrested and, the following day, was charged for attempting to extort money. Tunbridge re-visited Cream's lodgings to find a wealth of information.

On 22 June Matilda Clover's inquest was opened. Her body had been disinterred and analysed. It was riddled with strychnine. Dr Cream had been seen entering her premises on the day of her death. The jury brought the verdict that 'Matilda Clover died of strychnine poisoning and that the poison was administered by Thomas Neill Cream with intent to destroy life'.

Cream was tried at the Old Bailey on 17 October 1892. He was formally indicted for four murders and other crimes. There was no hard evidence but the Crown rested its

Cream's criminal career.

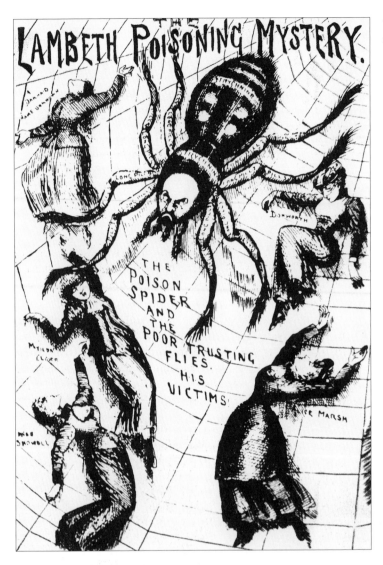

case on the cumulative evidence. The jury only took a few minutes to return a verdict of 'guilty'.

Had Cream not sent the letters, nor schemed for constant attention, his crimes might never have been detected. Could it have been his morphine habit that so addled his mind that he committed these murders?

He was hanged at Newgate on 15 November 1892. Legend has it that he uttered the infamous words 'I am Jack…' just as the rope cut his sentence short. Was he the Ripper or was it just one last attempt at being the centre of attention? Abberline, veteran of the Whitechapel murders and the 'Cleveland Street Scandal', affirmed that this was 'also another idle story. Neil Cream was not even in this country when the Whitechapel murders took place. No, the identity of the diabolical individual has yet to be established, notwithstanding the people who have produced these rumours and who pretend to know the state of the official mind.'

eleven

THE REAL DEMON BARBER

It was August 1901. Unemployed Maud Marsh, 18, of Croydon, answered an advert in the local paper for a barmaid at the Monument Tavern, Union Street, Borough. The landlord, a 34-year-old, imposingly mustachioed swarthy man with a hint of an American accent and something else, George Chapman, told her he was willing to take her on.

Mrs Marsh, Maud's mother, thought she should just check things out. She noticed Chapman had a wedding ring, Ah, Mrs Marsh thought, he was a widower and a family lived upstairs. The family were asked to leave soon after. Maud's parents were, however, impressed.

The neat Maud made quite an impression on Mr Chapman – or was it the opposite? A gift of a gold watch and chain was summarily written about in Maud's letters to her mother. Mrs Marsh was quite perturbed and warned her daughter.

Maud Marsh and George Chapman.

Chapman and Maud visited her family in Croydon, ostensibly to show that he was an honourable man. He told her parents that he wished to marry their daughter, and then showed them a will he had made in her favour. This he duly signed and it was witnessed by her brother.

The Marsh family weren't sure about Chapman's intentions. Her father visited, and then her mother, on Sunday 13 September. Confetti was strewn about the room. Maud explained that they had married that morning, 'Catholically', in a room in Bishopsgate. Where was the marriage certificate? Oh George had it.

The 'marriage' seemed to be highly volatile. Maud confided to her married sister, Louisa Morris, that 'you don't know what he is'. Yes George was masterful; he beat her and pulled her hair and yet she stayed with him.

In April 1902, Maud told her family that her husband had bought medicines including crystals to 'procure' an abortion.

In June 1902 Chapman took the lease of the Crown public house in the same street, but not before a fire had damaged the Monument Tavern and the insurance company had refused to pay up. Chapman took on a new barmaid, Florence Rayner. He asked Florence if she would like to go to America with him. When she said he had a wife, he retorted with, 'Oh I could give her that', clicking his fingers, 'and she would be no more Mrs Chapman.' Florence left in July, just before Maud started suffering from nausea, vomiting and diarrhoea.

Louisa Morris visited again, being told by Chapman that her sister was 'dying fast'. She insisted that something be done, so Chapman called a local doctor, Dr Stoker, but his ministrations seemed to have no effect. Her worried family insisted she went to Guy's Hospital. Maud was there from 28 July to 20 August, where, despite the doctors not knowing what was wrong with her, she made a full recovery.

Maud had only returned to the Crown for a short time when the symptoms re-occurred, but not before she and Mrs Morris had had tea together and Maud had confided that George had told her that she wouldn't live to see 28! Dr Stoker prescribed medicines, which the ever attentive Chapman prepared. Mrs Marsh visited several times, noticing that a brandy drink Chapman had left for his wife made her sick when she had a sip herself. On another visit, Chapman told another of Maud's sisters, Alice, that she could have a job as a barmaid when Maud died. She said it wasn't for her.

Finally, Mrs Marsh began to suspect Chapman. She and her husband asked their own doctor, Dr Grapel, to visit their daughter and consult with Dr Stoker. Dr Grapel was convinced she was being poisoned. It was too late – Maud died on 23 October.

Dr Stoker refused to grant a death certificate, much to Chapman's disgust. Stoker was in fact anxious enough to conduct a private post-mortem, requesting the analysis of the stomach and organs by the Chemical Research Association on Borough High Street. Their conclusion was that she had died from arsenic poisoning. Dr Stoker immediately wrote to the Coroner's Office and contacted the local police.

George Chapman was arrested on 25 October and charged with murder. The police searched the Crown and found a recently washed medicine bottle with traces of white powder, documents revealing Chapman's real name as Severin Klosowski and his date of birth, £300 in gold and notes, and medical books on poisons. A full post-mortem was made by the coroner, Dr Waldo, and the Home Office expert, Dr Thomas Stevenson. They revised the cause of death – poisoning by antimony.

But who was Chapman? Severin Antoniovich Klosowski was a 23-year-old Polish apprentice surgeon, with a fine record when he immigrated to Whitechapel, London, in 1888. There 'Ludwig' Klosowski was a hairdresser's assistant, moving to a barbershop in Tottenham, where he was known as 'Schloski'. He purchased another barbershop in the same locality and when that failed resorted to working in a barber's in Shoreditch and finally at a barber's in Church Lane in Leytonstone.

Whilst in the East End he had 'married' a young Polish girl, Lucie Badewski, had a child by her and was confronted by his 'original' Polish wife, who had come to find him. This *ménage à trois* did not last. One wife had to go – number one! The child died and the Klosowskis moved to America, only for Lucie to return alone in 1891, fed up with his philandering. He followed soon after only for her to leave him for good a few months later.

A highly-sexed man such as Klosowski could not remain single for long. Indeed, some women were drawn to this strong,

George Chapman.

almost dangerous man with a hint of cruelty. Annie Chapman (not one of the Ripper's victims) was to have two children by him. His womanising made her leave too. She left him her name, though, and in 1895 'George Chapman' was living with the Renton family in Leytonstone, paying court to their married daughter, Mary Isabella Spink. When the husband left, George got his woman and her £600 fortune. They moved to Hastings where, after a failed barbershop venture, he bought another premise where his wife's piano playing brought in customers by the dozen to have their 'musical shaves'. Whilst there he became friendly with a local chemist who sold him some tartar emetic, asking him to sign the poisons book as required by law.

They sold their concern and moved back to London. Chapman took on the lease of the Prince of Wales tavern in St Bartholomew's Square, off City Road. A Mrs Doubleday helped 'Mrs Chapman' at the bar, and it was then that the landlady became ill with diarrhoea and vomiting. Mrs Doubleday suggested a Dr Rogers to help but despite his medicines, prepared by Mr Chapman, Annie died in December 1897.

Within months Bessie Taylor had been taken on as a barmaid and become the next 'Mrs Chapman', only to fall ill shortly after. They moved to run a pub in Bishop's Stortford, returning to London where Chapman took on the lease of the Monument Tavern in Borough.

Bessie Taylor was a popular landlady, easy on the eyes, with a sense of humour and a good soul despite being ill. It came as a shock to the community when Dr Stoker was brought in to administer to her, only for her to die on 13 February 1901. Dr Stoker obligingly filled out a death certificate with 'exhaustion from vomiting and diarrhoea'. Mr Chapman could not run a pub without a barmaid. His advert brought Miss Maud Marsh.

An inquest on Maud Marsh's death was held on 28 October 1902. The exhumations of Mrs Spink and Bessie Taylor were ordered. It took longer for Bessie as she had been buried in her native Cheshire. The bodies were remarkably well preserved, usually a sign that there was a retardant such as a poison. Enough antimony was found in the two bodies to reveal that they had been murdered.

Chief Inspector Abberline, the policeman in charge of the Whitechapel murders, was convinced that George Chapman was the 'Ripper'. When DI Godley arrested Chapman he sent him a congratulatory note saying 'You've got the Ripper at last'.

What made Abberline think

George Chapman and Bessie Taylor.

this was the case? He had, during the 'Jack the Ripper' frenzy, closely interviewed Lucie Badewski. She had told him that her husband left the house for hours on end during the night. Chapman had, furthermore, arrived in Whitechapel at about the time of the first murder; the murders took place at a weekend, showing that the murderer had a regular job, as did Chapman; the description of the man seen with Kelly seemed to fit his; both seemed to have knowledge of medical procedure, and the murders stopped when Chapman left for America. There were two 'holes' in his arguments; could Chapman speak good English when he arrived? This was crucial to the Ripper investigation as sightings of the possible killer had always been followed by statements that the individual could speak English well. Would the *modus operandi* change so drastically from physical mutilation to poisoning? Some psychologists have always maintained that killers never change their method of killing; others say that experimentation leads to new avenues. 'Chapman' seemed to kill for money; Mrs Spink had a tidy fortune, Bessie Taylor was from a comfortable background and had been included in her father's will, while the young Maud also seemed to come from a solid middle-class family.

The trial was held on 11 February 1903 at the Central Criminal Court. Chapman was tried for the murder of Maud Marsh. Despite his continued assertions that he was George Chapman and American, the presiding judge, Mr Justice Grantham, refused to entertain this and sentenced him as Severin Klosowski after the jury had deliberated for barely ten minutes. He was hanged at Wandsworth Prison on 7 April 1903.

twelve

FOR THE LOVE OF A GOOD WOMAN

In 1897, Munyon's, the American Patent Medicine Company, sent a home-grown manager for their new branch in London. Dr Hawley Harvey Crippen was a mild-mannered, diminutive (he was only 5ft 4in), bespectacled, homeopathic doctor with a large, blousy wife named Cora.

He had been to England before, during his studies in 1882. He had attended various hospitals to watch operations and had done an elective at the Royal Bethlehem Hospital, where he also watched the effect a new drug, Hyoscine, had on difficult mental patients.

Dr Hawley Harvey Crippen.

He had returned to America the following year, graduating from university as a homeopathic doctor and as an ear and eye specialist. A blissful, though short, marriage to a nurse produced a son, Oscar, who was sent to live with his grandparents in California when his mother died. Dr Crippen, meanwhile, worked in New York, where he met and married the attractive and bubbly Cora Turner in 1892, only to discover her real name was Kunigunde Mackamotzki after the wedding. They tried for a child but a life-threatening illness meant that Cora had to have a hysterectomy. This would have far-reaching consequences. It left her scarred both emotionally and physically. She threw herself into singing lessons, which her husband obligingly paid for.

The couple settled in Bloomsbury, where Cora took up acting. Crippen, probably mortified by his wife's operation and its consequences, worked to please his wife – a mistake he would later rue. The bolster to her ego made her more demanding and the occasional sallies onto the boards, notably with another actor, Weldon Atherston, proved to be disastrous.

Cora became 'Belle Elmore' in 1899 and achieved a little more success, but not as much as she thought her talents deserved. By now Mrs Crippen was starting to fill out into a Rubenesque figure with a temper to match.

Her husband's sacking by Munyon's in 1900, probably caused by the company's belief that his professional management of his wife was incompatible with his job, gave him the opportunity to become consulting physician to several companies of the same ilk in London, one of which was Drouet's. It was there he met 18-year-old typist Ethel Le Neve and her sister. All three became good friends. Ethel Neave, to use her real name (she had adopted the more middle-class Le Neve), was the complete opposite of Belle. She was slim, young and pretty. She was also very lonely. The mutual loneliness would bring them together.

He never mentioned his wife except in passing and it was only in 1904 that Ethel met Belle officially – she was not impressed by the garrulous, overstuffed and overbearing dyed blonde wife.

The year 1905 proved a turning point. Munyon's took Crippen back. He brought Ethel with him as his secretary. He also marketed himself as an eye specialist and sold remedies from home. The Crippens moved to a large house at 39 Hilldrop Crescent, close to Camden tube. The house was perfect for Belle. It was a semi-detached house with a long and pretty back garden, a semi-basement and three floors. The rent was fractionally too high, but they rented out rooms until Belle tired of the extra work. It was also not far from Ethel.

An ex-lodger would later say that Crippen was 'extremely quiet and gentlemanly in thought and behaviour to his wife and everyone else'. He let her win at cards, collect various pets such as cats, birds and a bull terrier, to whom he was devoted. He also tolerated her becoming Honorary Treasurer of the Music Hall Ladies' Guild based at nearby Albion House, where, coincidentally, Crippen's office was located. Her ebullient

Belle Elmore.

Number 39 Hilldrop Crescent.

and jocular personality made her very popular with many variety hall artistes and her parties and dinners were not to be missed.

In December 1906, Ethel and the diminutive, shy, balding Dr Crippen became lovers. She, in particular, was attracted to the older man's kindness, empathy and generosity. He had found the woman he wanted to spend the rest of his life with. They called each other 'Hub' and 'Wifey' and were besotted with each other. Her miscarriage in 1908 made her feel particularly vulnerable, but although her lover was always there to make her feel better, he wasn't her husband. She met and disappeared with a chemist's clerk for five months, but returned to Crippen to prove her point.

Belle had guessed that her husband was in love with someone else and now only tolerated him.

He invited friends of hers, Paul and Clara Martinetti, for supper on Monday, 31 January 1910. It was a good evening; Mrs Crippen was a good cook. It was the last time Belle was seen alive.

In February, Ethel brought a letter to the Music Hall Ladies' Guild in Albion House. It tendered Belle's resignation as Treasurer, giving the excuse of family difficulties in America and her need to be there. It was in Dr Crippen's writing! Later that month Crippen attended the Music Hall Benevolent Fund dinner at the Criterion Restaurant, accompanied by Ethel in his wife's jewels. The Martinettis and others were shocked to see the jewels on another woman – they all wondered what had happened to Belle. Another couple, Mr and Mrs John Nash, went on a trip to New York and asked the whereabouts of Belle, only to receive a letter from Clara Martinetti saying that Crippen had told her his wife had died in Los Angeles. John Nash called the Los Angeles Police Department, to be told that no such person had died.

The Nashes' return to England brought more questions, which Crippen couldn't answer. A death notice for Belle in the *Stage* magazine convinced Nash to visit Scotland Yard. Meanwhile, the Guild had sent a letter to Crippen's son in California, only to receive a reply saying that his father had told him of his stepmother's death. Chief Inspector Walter Dew, who had cut his teeth on the Whitechapel murders, would be assigned the case in July.

Dew was thorough. He checked with the Guild and saw the letters sent by Crippen. He then checked the Crippens' financial affairs and finally called on Crippen with a colleague, Mitchell, at Hilldrop Crescent on Friday 8 July. A French maid answered the door, Ethel Le Neve followed soon afterwards only to say she was the housekeeper when they introduced themselves. She offered to fetch Crippen from his office at Albion House but the police insisted upon accompanying her.

Chief Inspector Walter Dew.

Crippen was only too pleased to set the record straight. He admitted that he thought that his wife was alive. His statement seemed to ring true. On their arrival in England his wife kept criticising him and telling him he was not good enough for her. She developed an attachment with an American actor, Bruce Miller, who had since returned to America. Their marriage had become increasingly difficult and, after an argument when the Martinettis visited in January, she had left him the next day. He had covered her absence to avoid scandal, written letters, told of death and even placed an obituary in the *Stage* magazine. He suspected she may have joined Bruce Miller.

The statement was so long that Dew invited Crippen to an Italian restaurant for lunch, where Crippen tucked into a steak with great gusto. Crippen admitted his affair with Ethel, giving her some of his wife's jewels, and living together in his house.

They then interviewed Ethel. She was surprised to hear of Belle's death, but knew that the marriage was fractious. A quick check of the house revealed nothing. Dew and his colleague left late but not before Crippen had offered to have an advert placed in the American papers for his missing wife.

A description of Belle was telegraphed to all the London police stations and Dew returned to Albion House on Monday 11 July. Crippen and Ethel had gone! Crippen's assistant, Long, explained that Crippen had arrived early on the 9th, asked him to go out to buy some boys' clothes and cashed a cheque with the manager. Crippen and Le Neve left by 1 p.m. Both Long and Dr Rylance, a colleague of Crippen's, had received letters that evening to wind up his household affairs. The house keys were enclosed.

Dew and Mitchell arrived at Hilldrop Crescent to find Mrs Long there. She had found the discarded draft of the advert for the American papers under the sofa. Once again the house revealed nothing. An all-points bulletin was sent to all ports at home and abroad and the policemen returned the next morning to search and question the neighbourhood, with no luck.

On Wednesday 13 July, Dew and Mitchell returned to the house, dug up the garden and checked the coal cellar under the front steps. A loose brick in the floor made them dig up the rest. There they found what they thought were human remains. They called for help from Kentish Town police station and two more policemen came to help. Some kitchen cleaner was used to keep the stench at bay, without adulterating the crime scene.

Augustus Pepper, a consultant surgeon, Dr William Wilcox, a toxicologist, and Bernard Spilsbury, a pathologist, arrived on Thursday. Certain items were recognisable: tufts of dark brown hair in a curler and small pieces of short, fair hair. The remains were taken to the mortuary and analysed.

It was the remains of a torso. It had been expertly filleted; only part of a thigh bone was discovered. The torso had belonged to a stout person and the dissector must have had an exceptional knowledge of human anatomy. A piece of flesh with what looked like marks corresponding to a scar and pubic hairs indicated that the person was female and had had their ovaries removed. Some of the hair was bleached but its roots were naturally brown – over the weeks the hair would resume its normal colour. Another piece of evidence was the remains of a pyjama jacket with the shop label 'Jones' in the collar. Lack of grey hairs indicated a young or middle-aged adult. The remains, despite the lime, had been in the cellar between four and eight months. Spilsbury eventually came to the conclusion that it was an old scar and a microscopical examination proved this. But how did this person die? William Wilcox would discover how.

Meanwhile the police issued descriptions of the two fugitives and sent wanted posters. The Home Secretary offered a £250 reward and the Press surmised. Two officers had spoken to an officer of a Canadian ship, the *Montrose*, bound for Canada via Antwerp, on Thursday 14 July, giving a full description of Crippen as a possible clergyman and Le Neve as a boy. The ship's captain saw a man and a boy boarding the ship at Antwerp and noticed how the boy squeezed the man's hand. It didn't seem quite right to him. They were a father and son from Detroit. After he had talked to the man about seasickness the captain was convinced the man was the fugitive doctor and telegraphed Scotland Yard. Dew, in strict secrecy, took a faster steamer, the *Laurentic*, from Liverpool.

Dressed as a pilot, Walter Dew arrested Crippen and Le Neve at Quebec as the *Montrose* docked on 31 July. Crippen had already made a favourable impression on Dew. Dew realised that here was one of life's tragedies – a decent, lonely, gentle hen-pecked man who had finally met someone who loved him for himself. The journey home was uneventful, except for the media attention. They arrived back on Saturday 27 August.

By then the toxicologist, William Wilcox, had found evidence that would seal Crippen's fate. Sealed samples had been left at the mortuary in mid-July. Dr Wilcox found enough Hyoscine in the remnants to kill. It had been taken by mouth and death would have occurred in an hour. The experiment was repeated and the findings confirmed. Judicious enquiries revealed that Crippen had purchased, on behalf of Munyon's, 5 grains of Hyoscine hydrobromide from a chemist on New Oxford Street on 19 January 1910. Munyon's, however, never used Hyoscine – its drugs were made in America and shipped to England.

The two would be tried independently. Crippen's trial was held on Tuesday, 18 October 1910. Arthur Newton, of Cleveland Affair fame, said he would act for him without a fee.

Crippen and Le Neve in court.

His counsel was Alfred Tobin, whilst the prosecution's counsel was Richard Muir. On hearing that Muir was to be his prosecutor, Crippen remarked, 'I wish it had been anybody else … I fear the worst.' And indeed it was! The prosecution had even paid for Bruce Miller and Belle's sister to be brought to England. Whilst there was no definite proof that Crippen had killed his wife, the array of circumstantial evidence expertly sealed his fate. The prosecution had to have his guilt established by association. Bruce Miller refuted any impropriety with Belle and her sister remembered the scar Belle had after her hysterectomy. Jones Brothers had sold two pairs of pyjamas, of an identical pattern to the remnant found with the remains, to Mrs Crippen in 1909. The defence tried to prove that the scar was a fold, and was from the buttock, but the pubic hair disproved this.

The jury took twenty-seven minutes to find Crippen guilty. He was moved to Pentonville and hanged on 23 November. He always maintained he was innocent.

Ethel was tried as an accessory to the crime four days after Crippen was found guilty. Crippen had always maintained she was totally innocent of any wrongdoing. Her jury thought the same.

Had Crippen really killed his wife? No one knows for sure. A letter was sent to him from America whilst he was awaiting his sentence, but never opened. If he did administer the Hyoscine to his wife, was it just to make her sleep so he could see his mistress? Had he misjudged the amount and then panicked when he found her dead? At least he died in the knowledge that someone he loved, loved him back.

thirteen

THE FINAL CURTAIN

In the same week that Dew and Mitchell uncovered the remains of a body in Dr Crippen's coal cellar at 39 Hilldrop Crescent, Camden in 1910, another drama unfolded at 17 Clifton Gardens, Battersea, in South London.

At 9.30 p.m., Saturday, 16 July 1910, Edward Noice, a chauffeur, was driving along Rosenau Road, Battersea, when he heard two gunshots. He looked in the direction of the shots and saw a man scaling the garden wall of a house off Clifton Gardens, Prince of Wales Road, and running towards the Thames. He drove to the nearest police station to report the incident. An officer was despatched to the house, 17 Clifton Gardens, and spoke to the tenant of the flat next door, a very attractive young woman named Elizabeth Earle.

Both Miss Earle and her dinner guest, 21-year-old Thomas Frederick Anderson, confirmed hearing gunshots and glimpsing a prowler as he vaulted over the garden wall. Anderson had rushed to the darkened flat next door, seen a sprawled body at the foot of the stairs and had alerted the local police.

Searching the garden at the back of the building, the officer heard heavy breathing and followed the sound to the foot of an interconnecting external staircase between the two buildings.

There, sprawled on the ground, lay a fully-clothed man in slippers, dying of a bullet wound to the head. The policeman searched the dying man's pockets, finding a life preserver (in this case a piece of insulated electric cable, looped at one end for the wrist, wrapped in paper and wool), a bus ticket from King's Cross and a calling card identifying the bearer, one Thomas Weldon Atherston.

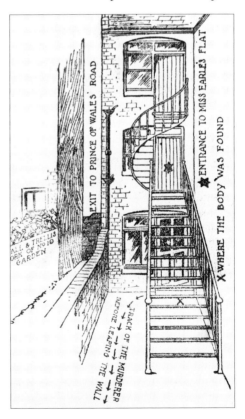

Plan of Clifton Gardens.

A more detailed search was made later, identifying imprints of a size 9 boot in the soft earth by the wall of the property and a spent bullet found in the woodwork of the scullery door of the empty flat.

The policeman returned to Miss Earle's flat and asked whether she or her guest knew a Mr Atherston. At the mention of this name, Mr Anderson blanched. It was his father's stage name! He then identified the body as that of his father. What, though, was Mr Anderson senior doing in bedroom slippers, and why did his son not immediately recognise him?

The story was certainly bizarre! Thomas Anderson was a trained actor, a bad one, with four children (two boys and two girls). His stage name was Weldon Atherston. He had been moderately successful in the dying

Thomas Weldon Anderson, aka Weldon Atherston.

decades of the nineteenth century, but his age and, quite frankly, lack of acting skills, made him leave his wife and take up with a much younger and impressionable actress, Elizabeth Earle, in 1900. He got the occasional jobs, including reciting poems in a booming, over-dramatic style in third- or even fifth-rate venues.

Elizabeth, meanwhile, had realised that money could be made in teaching acting, rather than doing it, and made a comfortable living out of it from her flat in Battersea. Anderson made less and less. Arguments followed and he left, staying with his sons, William and Frederick, in Percy Street, King's Cross. Frederick met Elizabeth and they became friends. Was it just a friendship?

A murder it certainly was ... but questions asked by the police remain unanswered to this day. What business did Anderson have with his father's ex-mistress? Did Earle and Anderson conspire to murder Atherston? Who was the gunman seen fleeing Earle's garden after the fatal shots were fired? What were the marks on the wrists of the dead man?

The police seem to have established that Earle was more of a mother to the Atherston boys and regularly ate with Thomas. Weldon Atherston was certainly paranoid and had become increasingly so since a head injury in 1908 when he had fallen off a bus. He was also insanely jealous of Miss Earle and had taken to spying on her. Entries in his diary suggested that and more. One entry read, 'Watched the lights until 11.30 when the lights went out.' Another ran 'found bunch of flowers in the ashbin', a present Miss Earle categorically denied receiving. A significant passage in his diary read:

> ...if he had kept away from her, if he had broken from the spell of her fascination and remained out of reach, this would have never happened. He has no one to thank but himself. We all reap as we have sown.

Many entries in the diary referred to love and to personal observations on Miss Earle. Most details of her daily life were recorded. It was certainly the diary of a jealous man. But why was he wearing slippers, and why was he found in a darkened flat?

What the police surmised was that the marks on the dead man's wrists showed that he had been held by a very strong individual while another may have shot him. Three witnesses saw a man running away from the flat down Rosenau Road. One described the unknown man as about 30, 5ft 5ins tall with a moustache and bowler hat. Another described a man by the river running from Rosenau Road, but with no moustache. Certainly the boot prints were not the same size as Thomas Anderson's.

The police were at a loss to explain this. An article on the murder was placed with the *New York Times* on 22 August 1910 with an appeal for information, but none was forthcoming. One fact, though, was that this part of Battersea had been plagued by a spate of burglaries – maybe Atherston had tried to stop one? This murder in genteel Battersea was unfortunately overshadowed by the more shocking one at Hilldrop Crescent (*see* chapter 12).

By a strange twist of fate the Atherston and Crippen cases had something in common. Atherston took on the job of entertainer in a Vaudeville show in 1907. The roster of entertainers also showed another performer, a certain Belle Elmore, whose singing voice was as questionable as Atherston's talent. Both were booed off the stage. Belle Elmore was the stagename of Cora – Mrs Hawley Crippen!

Elizabeth Earle moved to France and Thomas Anderson to New Zealand. On his deathbed, Anderson admitted to an £8,000 fraud!

The Enquiry.

fourteen

MAY GOD HAVE MERCY ON YOUR SOUL

It was at Parkhurst Prison that the notorious conman, Harry Benson (1866-1917), met and befriended Steinie Morrison, the supposed killer of Leon Beron on Clapham Common in 1911. Benson was serving a five-year sentence for fraud and would be released in 1914.

A number of influential people thought that Morrison was innocent. Benson, seizing the moment, started claiming that he was starting a fund to set Morrison free. Once his sentence finished, however, he set about financing a fine lifestyle for himself! One gullible wealthy woman even gave Benson £5,000 to start a weekly newspaper that he claimed would be used to free Morrison. The more he asked the more she gave. In one instance, he bought a farm and hired some ex-convicts to work on it, bringing the woman down to see how he was helping to rehabilitate prisoners. This scheme was very successful and the proceeds were to afford Benson a fine lifestyle. Even Morrison was taken in, sending him letters of encouragement – unfortunately for Morrison, Benson died in 1917, just as he was about to be arrested for this massive and most successful fraud.

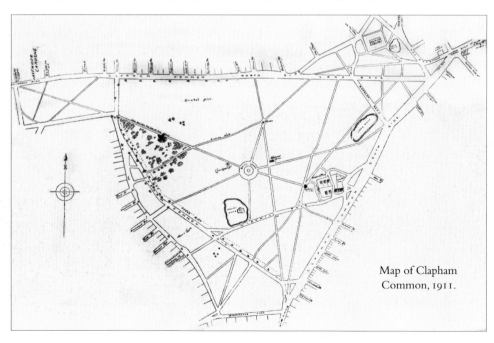

Map of Clapham Common, 1911.

Steinie Morrison's crime was the most high-profile case of the early twentieth century. It not only permeated the East End and some of its most insalubrious natives, but it also brought the East End to genteel Clapham. The first of a series of crimes that have since made Clapham no stranger to controversy.

It was the battered body of the slum landlord Leon Beron, found in some bushes off the west side path of Clapham Common, leading to Lavender Gardens, early in the morning of New Year's Day 1911, that eventually led the police to their prime suspect – Steinie Morrison.

PC Joseph Mumford was walking along the railed path past the woods when he noticed a trail of blood that led to a patch of flattened grass, where the body of a man had been dragged. There, with a handkerchief over the face, lay the body of a middle-aged man shrouded in a thick black coat. Mumford hurried to Cavendish Road police station.

The man had suffered heavy blows to his head with an angled instrument, had several stab wounds to his chest and bore two s-shaped cuts on his cheeks. Cards on his person established his identity.

Leon Beron was also a fence and habitually kept £30 on his person and carried a fob watch. Both money and the watch were missing. He lived in the East End, ate regularly at the Warsaw Restaurant – known as Snellwars after its owner – and had last been seen with Steinie Morrison the night before, according to various sources. Both men knew Clapham; Beron's father was in accommodation down Nightingale Lane and Morrison used to work in Lavender Gardens. Morrison was arrested within a week, just as he was tucking into a meal at a restaurant in Whitechapel on 8 January.

The court case, which took place on 6 March 1911, was one of the most baffling ever. Not for the lack of witnesses, but the very opposite – and most, for the defence or the prosecution, were completely at variance with each other. Even the accused, whose aliases confused even more (Morris Stein, Moses Tagger, Alexander Petropavloff), was to dispute his place and date of birth. What we do know is that he was aged between 28 and 32, was Jewish, had been in England for at least ten years, spoke good English and was out on licence for a previous misdemeanour. He was a petty crook, and lived in the East End. He bought and sold cheap jewellery, did a bit of thieving and had also worked as a baker in Lavender Gardens. He had bought a revolver in Aldgate under the name of

The body of Leon Beron.

Where the murder took place.

Petropavloff. He was also the last man to have been seen with the deceased, at Snellwars' restaurant. They had both spent the major part of the day together.

Morrison was a personable and pleasant young man who was quite candid about his lifestyle and previous convictions. He also spoke well. On his arrest he immediately told the arresting officer, Inspector Wensley (who had been involved, in a minor role, in the Whitechapel murders), that it was for murder. This was seen as a confession of sorts until a police constable eventually admitted that it was he who had told Morrison what he was being arrested for. It was hardly an auspicious start for the prosecution! The irony was that he had only been arrested because he had failed to notify the authorities of a change of address. As a prisoner on remand he was required to do so. He had moved from his digs in the East End to Lambeth on 1 January, although he had told his landlady he was going to Paris. Maybe he had said this so as not to offend her – something he later mentioned in court.

Leon Beron.

Two witnesses retracted their previous statements. Eva Flitterman stated, on 1 January, that she had seen a £5 watch on Morrison but later retracted her statement when she realised that it was not the same as her father's – Morrison's had a Kruger half sovereign. A boy at the Police Court, Rosen, swore he had seen Morrison with a revolver at 1.30 a.m. on 1 January, but he later also retracted his statement.

Bloodstains on Morrison's collar and shirt at the time of his arrest seemed to imply that he was the killer. But why would he wear these a week after the crime, particularly as he had boxes of extra collars? Could it have been because he was prone to nosebleeds – a fact that was shown in court? Blood from an attack would have been far more widespread on his clothing.

He claimed that he had gone to the Shoreditch Empire at half past nine on the evening of 31 December 1910 – this was corroborated by Snellwar, a Jack Taw and the Brodsky family, but denied by the manager of the Empire. He couldn't remember what he had paid but he came back to his digs at about midnight, his landlord bolting the door after him – this was substantiated in court by his landlord. The iron bar (if indeed it was an iron bar he had brought to the restaurant the night before) did not have the same shape as the indentations on the head of the deceased.

The most telling evidence was that of three cabmen, Hayman, Stephens and Castlin, who had described their fare in great detail. Hayman swore he had picked up the accused and a smaller man at 2.30 a.m. from the Mile End corner of Sidney Street and taken them to Lavender Hill. He altered the time to 2 a.m. in a later statement, to fit in – otherwise he couldn't have picked him up. Stephens and Castlin had picked up Morrison at Clapham Cross and Kennington respectively. Both had seen Morrison's face in the papers prior to identifying him on 17 January and Stephens had not recognised Morrison's portrait. Could identification be made at that time of night?

Left & above: Steinie Morrison in the dock.

The problem with this trial was that according to the Criminal Evidence Act of 1884, no question may be put to the prisoner which tends to show previous bad character or convictions. This was not adhered to. It is also, even today, a common weakness of juries to think that a man is more likely to be guilty if he has been guilty of other crimes. The accused should be convicted solely on the evidence directly relevant to the crime he is charged with.

Finally, on 15 March, the presiding judge, Mr Justice Darling, aware that there was no direct evidence linking Morrison to the crime, said that there was reasonable doubt as to whether the evidence established the guilt of the prisoner. Thirty-five minutes later the jury gave its guilty verdict. A petition to the Home Secretary, Winston Churchill, commuted the death sentence to life imprisonment. The dejected Morrison, claiming his innocence to the end, starved himself to death, eventually dying in Parkhurst on 21 January 1921.

The arresting officer, Inspector Wensley, was to have an exceptional career, ending up as Chief Constable of the CID. His involvement in the Steinie Morrison case was, however, contentious, as he has been accused of trying to shepherd the witnesses to try to create a watertight case.

fifteen

TRUE TO YOURSELF

The following case would probably have been consigned to the dustbin of murder cases had it not been for an outcry from the Press at the disparity of the outcome of this trial and that of another.

Finborough Road, SW10, is a soulless, long traffic corridor in the West Brompton district with tall crumbling late Victorian/early twentieth century terraced houses. It was a street of relatively cheap housing within easy access to the centre of London and near to the Earl's Court tube station. The end of the First World War also saw the resurgence of serious crime caused, in part, by post-war deprivation and a serious case of demoralisation. This road would certainly court this.

Twenty-five-year-old Gertrude Yates had been a shopgirl in a furriers in the West End, but found that her looks and youth attracted a better class of gentlemen who would pay her well for more personal services in her basement flat, festooned with 'sateen weeping Pierrot dolls, shiny pots, reminders of daytrips to seaside resorts and sequinned greeting cards that were too pretty to throw away.' Olive Young, as she preferred to be called, earned enough money to employ a daily maid, Emily Steel, who also lived on the same road. She was, as she put it, 'a lady with male friends'.

Ronald True (1892-1951) was one of these 'male friends'. He was the epitome of a man with Byronic good looks. He was tall, dark and handsome with large eyes, an airman's moustache and more dash than cash. He was a twinkly-eyed gregarious man with a fund of stories about his Flying Corps

Ronald True.

76

days and his wealth. The reality was sad and desperate. He was a morphine addict, with violent mood swings, who had been invalided out of the Flying Corps following a very bad knock on the head.

Born to an unmarried young girl of 16 who had the good fortune to make a very advantageous marriage some eleven years later, Ronald went to the local grammar school. He had led a nomadic existence, with a liberal allowance from his mother, until the First World War, when he decided to join up. Despite failing most of his exams he managed to get his wings and, on the war's completion, went to America where his banter, lying and easy charm got him jobs and also lost him jobs. He also acquired a wife. His progressive morphine abuse made his already delicate mental balance even more fragile. He returned to England with his wife and continued his aimless existence, punctuated with frequent absences, to dream, lie, con and satisfy his increasing addiction to morphine.

Despite the birth of a son, his frequent absences made his family very uneasy. They were right to be so. His increasingly erratic forays into the London demimonde, signing dud cheques, stealing and leaving hotels without paying, made 'Major' True not just an embarrassment but a liability. His occasional returns enabled the family to have him sent for various cures – but to no avail. His addiction continued to spiral out of control, and affected his sense of reality. He invented an alter ego who was responsible for all his failings – possibly when his addled brain realised just how far he had degenerated. In short he was mad. His family even alerted Scotland Yard, with no success.

Olive and the 'Major' met for the first time on 18 February 1922. She took him back to her basement flat where he stayed the night, only to steal £5 from her purse on his departure. He had made her feel uneasy and the theft had made her resolve never to see him again.

She managed to elude him for two weeks despite his continuous telephone calls, but he finally caught up with her just before midnight on Sunday 5 March. She had just caught the tube back from Piccadilly Circus. Despite her misgivings, she let him in and they spent the night together. In the morning he made her a cup of tea and as she sat up in bed to drink it he struck her with a rolling pin, rammed a towel down her throat and strangled her with a dressing gown cord. He left her naked body in the bathroom and stole all the jewellery and cash he could find.

Ronald True, the aviator.

At about 9.15 a.m. Emily Steel, Miss Young's daily maid, arrived. She made herself a cup of tea and started tidying the sitting room. True appeared, smiling, and said that her mistress was asleep. She was not to be woken up and he would have her collected at about midday. She helped him on with his coat as he was leaving and he gave her half a crown. They both left together, he getting into his chauffeur-driven car, she to return about half an hour later.

Emily knocked on the bedroom door and walked in. She thought someone was sleeping in the bed, but on pulling back the counterpane she found two blood-soaked pillows placed vertically down the bed, and a bloodied rolling pin.

Hurrying out of the bedroom she looked in the bathroom, only to find her bloodied employer's body lying beside the bath. She phoned for the police, telling them about the chauffeur-driven car.

True continued the day as if nothing had happened, ending up at the Hammersmith Palace of Varieties in the evening, where he dismissed his driver, Mazzola. This man had been driving him around for several weeks and had yet to receive any payment. The police were waiting for Mazzola at his garage. He told them where he had dropped off Major True. Ronald True was arrested at the Hammersmith Palace of Varieties. Items of Miss Young's jewellery were found in his pockets. He was charged with wilful murder and his trial started on Monday, 1 May 1922.

The story, however, does not end here. Yes, here was a man who needed money. Miss Young had cash and valuables. He murdered her and stole what he could find. He sold what he could, changed his bloodied clothing and tried to avoid detection. This was an act that might be done by a sane man, not an insane one. This is what the police rested its case on.

It was, however, patently obvious to the police when they took him into custody that here was a very deranged and quite possibly insane man. He was placed under the care of Doctors East and Young at the Brixton Prison Hospital, where his sleeplessness and occasional outbursts of violence persuaded the doctors to give him sedatives. He was popular, though, with his fellow inmates, including one Henry Jacoby, but his delusions and highs and lows, followed by periods of intense agony and feelings of persecution, enabled separate medical opinions to judge him as insane. The prosecution was in a quandary. It had True examined by yet another expert, Dr Cole. Dr Cole declared that True was not insane, but with important reservations. The prosecution's course of action was to not have Cole put in the witness box but to rely on cross-examination and the application of the M'Naghten's Rules.

The M'Naghten's Rules are clearly defined for a plea of insanity; the jurors ought to be told in all cases that every man is presumed to be sane, and has sufficient mental faculties to be responsible for his crimes, until the contrary is proved to their satisfaction. It must be proved clearly, to establish a defence on the grounds of insanity, that at the time of committing the act, the accused was labouring under such a defect of reason, from disease of the mind, as not to know the nature and quality of the act he was doing; or if he did know it, that he did not know that what he was doing was wrong.

Despite a plea of insanity the jury found him guilty. The Court of Criminal Appeal found no different and the case was then referred to the Home Office. An independent medical panel reviewed the case and reinforced what previous doctors had opined – that the man was a true lunatic. True was accordingly removed to Broadmoor for life.

The public outcry over True's reprieve was caused by the death penalty meted out to 18-year-old Henry Jacoby five days before True's trial. Henry Jacoby had been sentenced

Henry Jacoby.

to death over the murder of an elderly lady guest in the hotel in which he worked. He had planned to steal her valuables when she was asleep but had been forced to silence her when he found her awake.

The jury who had found Jacoby guilty also made strong recommendations for mercy because of his youth. The public fully expected a reprieve due to Jacoby's age and the fact that his action was not premeditated. Jacoby, however, was hanged despite his solicitor pleading his case at the Home Office and a petition with thousands of names, including some of his jury, being handed in. The public and the Press thought this was a case of there being one law for the poor and one law for the rich. The Home Secretary was pilloried in the media and in Parliament.

The fact remained that True's state of mind was constantly referred to in court, whilst Jacoby's was not. True spent the rest of his life in Broadmoor, popular to the end.

sixteen

SAVED BY THE RAIN

Sir Richard Muir (1857-1924) was widely regarded as the greatest prosecutor of his time. He was originally a reporter for *The Times* newspaper but turned to law, becoming a Crown Prosecutor. He represented every notable trial until his death and was known for his meticulous research.

His methodology was quite simple and very laborious. He would make notes on small cards with different coloured pencils; one colour for examination in chief, one colour for cross-examination and so on. His card system became notorious in his department and with the police. He had little time for eyewitness testimony but relied on physical evidence and would always visit, and carefully annotate, the scene of crime. In one instance it would fail him miserably, because, for once, he did not follow his golden rule.

It was early evening on Wednesday, 9 May 1923. The West End was busy. People were returning from work and crowds were beginning to assemble for the evening's entertainment. Shaftesbury Avenue's Globe Theatre was showing 'Aren't We All', a delicious Lonsdale comedy starring Marie Lohr. The cab ranks were piling with empty cabs waiting for their fares.

Thirty-nine-year-old Jacob Dickey, a cab driver, was ranked outside the Trocadéro. A young man hailed him and asked to be taken to Brixton. It was a fateful and fatal journey for Mr Dickey.

Brixton's Baytree Road, a quiet shortcut from Brixton Hill to Acre Lane, is an innocuous road even nowadays. It boasts tidy two-storey terraced houses with small front and back gardens. That

Sir Richard Muir.

Above: Baytree Road.   *Right:* Jacob Dickey.

evening, however, its suburban calm was punctured by two gunshots. Furtive eyes behind the muslin curtains viewed a man running away from an open-doored cab – and a body lay on the ground.

A telephone call alerted the Brixton police. The cab was stationary in the middle of the street; the body, that of the unfortunate Jacob Dickey, lay on the ground, as did a bloodied suede glove, a gold-topped ebony cane, a jemmy wrapped in a newspaper, and the murder weapon – a pistol.

Witnesses saw a man running towards 28 Baytree Road and indeed, a torch was found on the ground of its open garage. Footprints in the back garden and scuff marks on the wall showed that a person had jumped over in a hurry. An elderly and frightened woman living at 15 Acre Lane had seen a man jump off the wall into her back garden. He had asked gruffly if he could go through her house to get to Acre Lane. She was too terrified to say no and he disappeared.

The police had some clues. The local Superintendent, Frank Carlin, told them to contact the local newspaper to print a photograph of the unusual cane, it might bring results. He wasn't wrong. A cane in those days was part of a man's wardrobe. This one, besides,

Superintendent Frank Carlin.

was a very unusual one. An informant rang in to say it looked very much like the cane of a small-time American crook going by the name of Eddie Vivian. He was a professional housebreaker who sometimes carried a gun. The informant had seen him in Soho with a similar stick.

Mr Vivian was found in Charlwood Street, Pimlico, in his girlfriend Hettie Colquhoun's flat. Once back in Brixton he recognised his cane and his torch. He was very candid in his interrogation. On 9 May he had been in bed with an upset stomach. He'd eaten some bad sardines on Sunday. He had lent the cane to a friend, 'Scottie' Mason.

His story was that 'Scottie' (Alexander), a 22-year-old from Lanarkshire, and a Canadian deserter from the First World War, was a good friend of his. They had both done a job and been caught and sent to prison but kept up their friendship. Mason had just got out of jail for another job the preceding Saturday and visited Vivian on Sunday. They made plans to do a few more burgling jobs and had done some reconnaissance in South London on Monday and Tuesday. They were to do a 'job' on Wednesday but Vivian's stomach was still too sore so he opted out. Mason decided to do the job on his own. He borrowed the stick 'to look posh', the gloves, the torch and the jemmy, and left Mason at 7.30 p.m. that evening.

Mason returned dishevelled, bloodied and dirty at 11.30 p.m., claiming that he had botched the job and 'shot a taxi driver'. He stayed the night and left the next morning.

Vivian was kept in police custody and on Saturday 12 May a police sergeant recognised Mason in the street and arrested him. Once at Brixton, Mason acknowledged that he had been arrested because of his connection with Vivian. They were both put in an identity parade on Sunday where the two ladies of 15 Acre Lane recognised Mason. Vivian was released and Mason pleaded his innocence at the Police Court but made no written statement.

Prior to the Old Bailey trial on 7 July 1923, the Crown Prosecutor, Sir Richard Muir, visited the scene of the crime but never got out of the car to check it because of heavy rainfall. He requested, instead, that a policeman take a scaled diagram of the scene.

The trial lasted four days. On the second day, Mason's legal aid counsel, Arthur Fox-Davies (also known for his books on heraldry), cross-examined Vivian. He put it to him that the pistol was his. Vivian refuted this. Fox-Davies continued his attack, suggesting that Vivian was not ill on Wednesday as he had eaten the sardines on Sunday. The whole story was concocted to allay Hettie's suspicions. Vivian refuted this too.

Vivian acknowledged buying the jemmy. Fox-Davies contended that Vivian used a shady taxi driver by the name of Jakey to take him to 'jobs'. Vivian denied knowing any taxi driver by that name, or knowing Jacob Dickey. Fox-Davies then suggested that once Hettie had left the flat, Vivian got dressed, arranged to meet Mason at the corner of Baytree

Mason, the murderer.

Road and hailed a cab at the Trocadéro. He then had an argument with the cab driver at Baytree Road and shot him. Vivian also disputed this.

Mason would later deny he had a pistol, saying that Vivian had showed him one on Monday at which Mason had said, 'I won't work with anyone who's got a gun'. He also maintained he had tried to stop Hettie worrying and told her that Vivian was ill on Wednesday. Mason also said that he had waited for Vivian at Baytree Road, saw him arriving with the cab driver, heard the quarrel, saw Vivian jump out with the cabbie in hot pursuit and then heard the gunshots. Mason then ran, climbing over the front wall of 28b Baytree Road and into the garage yard. He heard Vivian ask for help, as his legs were injured, but Mason thought better of it and ran on through the house at 15 Acre Lane.

When Mason arrived back at the flat Vivian was there. Vivian explained that he had climbed over some garden walls into a street, mingled with crowds and taken a taxi from Kennington Road. Jacob Dickey's sister was brought to the stand and refused to countenance that her brother was dishonest.

Vivian's evidence was the prosecution's sole weapon. After a four-day trial the jury took just seventeen minutes to find Mason guilty. His appeal was also dismissed. The Home Secretary, William Bridgeman, however, thought that there was enough room for doubt and reprieved Mason five days before his execution.

There had, it transpired, been an error in court. The police had been negligent. The tracing of Baytree Road and Acre Lane was inaccurate and out of date. The constable charged with the drawing had taken the tracing from the Ordnance Survey without checking for any changes. The map had shown an opening between the houses fronting Acre Lane at the back of the garage yard through which Vivian and Mason could easily escape. The opening no longer existed! It had been fully blocked by a new building, meaning Vivian could never have got out if he had been injured.

Sir Richard Muir was also at fault. He hadn't examined the area properly because of the rainstorm. He had returned to the scene of crime after the trial and realised his mistake:

Good Lord, if only I had seen this earlier I could have proved that Vivian never got away in the way Mason said he did. If the Home Secretary reprieves Mason the fellow will get away with his life because of a thunderstorm!

Mason was released in 1937, served as a merchant seaman in the Second World War and was drowned when his ship was torpedoed.

seventeen

THE BLACKOUT RIPPER

The 1941 Blitz on London saw the implementation of safety measures designed to make London and other major cities lesser targets. One of the main measures was the 'blackout' of lights when night came. It afforded some measure of safety and some form of solace.

The blackout was also a perfect way for some enterprising Londoners to make money or continue in their transgressions without too much bother from the police. Some criminals were to take advantage of the situation by committing murder. One of the classic examples of the wartime murders is that of Rachel Dubinsky, whose partly burnt body was found under a stone slab in the grounds of a severely bomb-damaged Baptist church in Kennington. Patient detective work eventually convicted her killer – the harassed separated husband.

Montague Place air-raid shelter was no place to hide on the cold Sunday of 9 February 1942. Harold Batchelor discovered the body of a dark-haired, slender woman lying on her back, her ripped skirt hiked up to the thighs, her underwear stained with blood and her right breast exposed. She had only died a few hours before, from strangulation. There were no clues as to her identity or to the killer, except, as the chief of the Police Fingerprint Department, Detective Superintendent Frederick Cherrill, stated, when viewing the bruising on the neck, the killer was left-handed. Immediate investigations led to an emptied handbag a few streets away, followed by a painstaking door-to-door search that finally led to the woman's identification: Evelyn Hamilton, a pharmacist, who had rented a room for the night in a local lodging house. Sir Bernard Spilsbury's post-mortem revealed that she had eaten beetroot for her last supper. Later investigations revealed that she had eaten at the Lyons Corner House at Marble Arch late the previous night and had indeed consumed beetroot – this

Evelyn Hamilton.

placed her death in the early hours of the morning.

Two meter readers came to empty the meters early in the morning of 10 February at 153 Wardour Street. The front door of Evelyn Oatley's flat was slightly ajar. Her neighbour, Ivy Poole, was surprised because she knew that her friend 'worked nights' and liked to sleep in. She had brought an attractive military man late the night before and the noise of her radio had been quite deafening at times. The blackout curtains were still up so one of the meter men put his torch on. He ran straight out to find a policeman.

Inspector John Hennessey was just doing his rounds of Wardour Street when the meter man ran out. The bubbly, slim blond was dead. Her body was splayed across her bed with her throat slashed,

Evelyn Oatley.

jagged cuts near her pubic area and her own torch rammed inside her. A broken piece of mirror from her empty handbag, a bloodied tin opener and a pair of blood-smeared curling tongs were bagged and taken for testing. Spilsbury had nothing to add, but Cherrill's search for prints revealed a thumbprint on the mirror and prints on the tin opener, all made by the left hand. There was, however, no reason for them to think it was the same killer.

The newly divorced 30-year-old Mary Heywood was waiting, drink in hand, for her army officer boyfriend at the Universelle Brasserie on the corner of Jermyn Street and Haymarket. They were meeting between 8 and 9 p.m. that evening, Thursday 12 February.

While she was waiting she was approached by a well-spoken, good-looking young airman. He offered her a drink and then suggested they have a bite to eat at the Trocadéro. Slightly reluctant, she told him she was waiting for her boyfriend. He said it would be quick. It was. They only had a drink, as she had to get back. He asked and she gave her number, adding that she wasn't easy. He then insisted on escorting her back to the Brasserie. Picking up his gasmask holder he took her round a back route, cornered her into a dark alley and started choking her.

A young night porter saw the scuffle and a flashing light. He shouted as a man ran past him. He picked up her handbag and a gasmask holder and helped the bloodied and shaken young woman to the Saville Row police station. It was a service gasmask, not hers, and the service number on the holder was traced to one Air Cadet Gordon Frederick Cummins at St James's Close, Regent's Park. The police requested to see the man in question.

Later that evening, part-time prostitute and married 25-year-old blond Catherine Mulcahy was standing outside Oddendino's café in Piccadilly when she was accosted by a young airman. They agreed a price, £2, and took a cab to a flat near Marble Arch. The man then tried to choke her. She had the presence of mind to knee him where it hurt and run out of the flat screaming. A neighbour opened his door and both of them watched as the airman calmly put his clothes back on, left a further £8 in £1 notes, and left.

On Friday 13 February, 15-year-old Barbara Lowe reached her mother's flat at 9-10 Gosfield Street at 4.30 p.m. She was a boarder at a school outside London and spent her weekends with her single mother. What she didn't realise was that her well-dressed, well spoken, middle-aged mother paid the school fees with her earnings as a prostitute. 'The Lady', as she was known, operated alone. There was no answer at the flat but the next-door neighbour called her into his, where two policemen were waiting for her.

A war-time gasmask.

It transpired that a package had been left outside Margaret Lowe's flat for two days. The neighbours had been worried and called the police. Once Barbara was there the police kicked the front door in and, finding the bedroom door locked, kicked that in too. Mrs Lowe had been strangled with a stocking.

Once DCs Cherrill and a colleague had arrived they found more. Pulling the sheets back showed the carnage. Her abdomen had been torn open, revealing the intestines and other organs. There were cuts all around the groin and a wax candle had been pushed up the vagina. Various bloodied kitchen knives were on the sheets and there were prints on a half-filled tumbler and a candlestick holder. The right hand print on the candlestick holder established that the killer was left-handed, not unlike the Oatley killer – in fact they were identical! Spilsbury thought that the killer was a 'savage sexual maniac'. Mrs Lowe had possibly been killed on the 11th.

The papers were to dub the killer the 'Blackout Ripper'. He hadn't finished yet though. That same evening Henry Jouannet, the elderly manager of the Royal Court Hotel, returned at 7 p.m. to the flat he shared with his much younger wife, the statuesque, blond Doris, at 187 Sussex Gardens, Bayswater. The milk was still out, the bedroom door was locked and there was no answer. Fearing the worst, that she had reverted back to prostitution (which she had), he called the police. They smashed the bedroom door down to find a bloody mess. Doris was naked. She had been choked with a stocking. The flesh beneath her left breast was cut away and the genitals had been stabbed repeatedly. There were fingerprints on a hand mirror, bedroom door and wardrobe doors. Cherrill was convinced that this was the same person who had killed Oatley and Lowe. Furthermore, the prints matched.

Gordon Cummins.

Gordon Frederick Cummins was arrested at St James's Close, Regents Park, for the attack on Miss Heywood. He matched Catherine Mulcahy's description of her assailant: well-spoken, average height, light brown hair, moustache and grey/green eyes. His prints, furthermore, matched those held by the police and finally a piece of mortar found on the base of his gasmask holder matched that at the Montague Place air-raid shelter. A search of his belongings found several items belonging to his victims.

The married Cummins categorically denied everything. His wife wouldn't believe what he had done. His fellow cadets, although irked by his airs and graces, for which he was nicknamed the 'Count', couldn't believe it either. The facts, though, spoke for themselves.

His trial on Thursday, 4 April 1942 was for the murder of Evelyn Oatley. The jury only took thirty-five minutes to find him guilty. He was hanged during an air raid on 25 June 1942 at Wandsworth Prison.

eighteen

REGGIE'S REVENGE

It was on the train into London that Eileen Evans had seen the 'For Rent' board on the top-floor flat of 10 Rillington Place in early 1948. It was the perfect location for her brother, Timothy, and his pregnant wife Beryl. It was barely ten minutes' walk from the family home at St Mark's Road, Notting Hill.

The diminutive 23-year-old Timothy (he was only just above 5ft), and his 18-year-old bride moved into the top-floor flat of the dilapidated house in Easter 1948. They were an ill-assorted couple. He was an engaging Welsh van driver with 'educational difficulties'. She was a pretty, vivacious telephonist.

The house was divided into three 'flats'. The ground-floor flat was occupied by the Christies, a middle-aged childless couple from Yorkshire, and the first-floor flat was held by Mr Kitchener, an elderly misogynist. Kitchener seemed a typical grumpy old man whilst the Christies, to the young couple, were very friendly. Mr Christie, a tall, bespectacled, balding man of about 50, worked at Ultra Radio, was an ex-policeman and First World War veteran, while Ethel Christie worked at the Osram factory.

Eileen Evans, who helped the young couple redecorate their flat, found John Reginald Halliday Christie repulsive, as did most women, especially as he wore plimsolls so he could pad about unheard. Something about him made her skin crawl, and well it might! Christie was undoubtedly highly intelligent but had been brought up in an austere household dominated by a very Victorian and successful father

No. 10 Rillington Place.

John Reginald Christie.

Christie, the Special Constable.

and older sisters who mothered the sensitive boy, to his detriment. He was a mathematician whose school career was punctuated with little academic success. The female-dominated Christie household was to have a profound effect. His first sally into the world of sex was disastrous, earning him the nickname of 'Reggie No Dick'. His grandfather's death and his ensuing visit to the body were to give him a fascination for the morbid.

His joining the army was no less torturous. Fear of death and the effects of mustard gas were to make this sensitive and highly neurotic young man lose his voice. Once invalided out of the army he met and married Ethel, the daughter of neighbours. His twenties were punctuated by acts of violence, which led to a police record and the breakdown of his marriage. He moved to London in 1924, hoping that a clean break would give him some emotional independence. It apparently worked. He had a couple of relationships, albeit with prostitutes, hit one with a cricket bat during a quarrel and was imprisoned for six months. He was imprisoned again after being caught stealing a car.

While serving his sentence in 1933, he asked his wife to join him in London – after a nine-year absence. She did! They took a flat at the run-down 10 Rillington Place in Notting Hill and he signed on with the local doctor, Dr Odess.

Shortly after the beginning of the Second World War, Christie became a Special Constable in the Reserve Police. The resumption of marital relations did not seem to affect his roving eye – he had an affair in 1943 only to be discovered by the cuckolded husband in *flagrante delicto* and beaten up severely. This reinforced his fear of violence. He could not stand up to male dominance and was to take sweet revenge.

Revenge took the shape of a 21-year-old German part-time prostitute he had come to know through his job. With his wife in Sheffield on a brief break, Christie invited Ruth Fuerst back to his flat, strangled her during sex and bundled her body under the floorboards of the front room when his wife telegrammed that she was coming home early, with her brother. The brother was to sleep, unknowingly, next to a corpse for the night.

Christie interred Fuerst in his garden the following night.

He left the police force in 1944 to work for Ultra Radio and became friendly with the respectable catarrh sufferer Muriel Eady. Muriel and her boyfriend were to become good friends of the Christies. Little did she know that she was being groomed for his next fix! Indeed, sex for Christie was domination, and killing was the ultimate domination, giving him an inner calm he could not otherwise have. His visits to his doctor became more frequent when he needed his next fix. It was easy for him to arrange a sick note for the times when he decided to kill again.

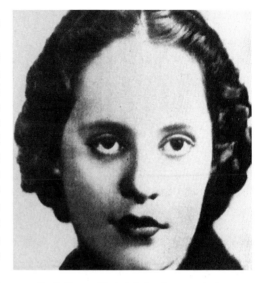

Ruth Fuerst, Christie's first known victim.

Ethel had her next trip to Sheffield in the autumn of 1944. Christie invited Muriel to the flat to try out an inhaler to alleviate her catarrh. He had woven an intricate tapestry of lies about his medical knowledge, especially in conjunction with the police. It was to be the last time she was ever seen. She arrived at the flat one day in early October. He showed her the inhaler with two tubes, placed it on her face and while she was inhaling the Friars balsam from one tube he gassed her with the other. He carried her to the bedroom and strangled her during sex. He would later bury her body in the garden. She was to be considered yet another victim of the German bombs.

The largely working-class neighbours were impressed with the middle-class Christie with his service in the Great War and with the police. Men tended to find him pleasant and intelligent and his hobby, photography, gave him quite a reputation. He also had another less salubrious hobby, collecting female pubic hairs – he now had two sets! A lonely man, he would talk to many people, and one, Mr Hookway, a furniture dealer on Portobello Road, became quite a chum.

Beryl Evans liked Mrs Christie. The Christies were quiet but always helpful. Reginald certainly liked Beryl, and unknown to all at 10 Rillington Place, he had made a peep hole in the wall to view the comings and goings.

Timothy Evans was an engaging character. Shortly after Timothy's birth his biological father left, never to return. His mother had remarried, to a Mr Probert, and moved the growing family from Wales to London: St Mark's Road, Notting Hill. It was a close-knit family. Timothy could not read or write, was educationally sub-normal but had a zest for life, managed to find a good job as a van driver and was liked by all. He was also a liar par excellence! His very fertile and largely innocuous imagination would give an Italian Count for his father and a brother with a fleet of cars, among other tall stories!

Beryl was gloriously pretty but an ineffectual housewife. The flat was perpetually dirty and their little daughter, Geraldine, who arrived in October 1948, was unwashed but well fed. Their early days were very happy and their daughter made their happiness even more precious. A friend said that 'they were a lovely couple, very fond of each other. Yes, they did quarrel a bit but never badly and never for long. They both thought the world of Geraldine.'

There were, however, some potentially serious cracks in the Evans' marriage: Beryl could not manage money and overspent: she invited a friend, Lucy, to stay at the flat, only for her husband to quarrel with her, leaving with Lucy and returning, tail between his legs, to his wife the following day.

Beryl became pregnant again in 1949. They could not afford another child and she desperately looked for ways to abort. She told the Christies. This was the perfect chance for Christie. He began grooming the impressionable Beryl for death, with precision. His chance came when Mr Kitchener had to be hospitalised for five weeks in October. Christie complained about the state of the house to the council and the owners were asked to deal with it. The builders, Mr Phillips, Fred Jones, Fred Willis and Robert Anderson moved in on 3 October 1949. Timothy wanted nothing to do with the abortion but Beryl pressed ahead, especially when Christie said he could do it at home. He explained to Timothy that he had done several before and was semi-trained to be a doctor anyway! The simple Timothy believed him.

After a quarrel with her husband, Beryl told him she and the baby were going down to Brighton the next day. He fully expected her to have gone when he returned from work but she had talked it over with Christie and she would have her abortion the next day, Tuesday 8 November. Christie arranged for a sick note from his doctor.

This time the gas panicked the patient in the kitchen. Christie had to resort to violence, strangled her and then had sex with her, only to find that a friend of Beryl's, Mrs Vincent, was trying to get into her kitchen. He wedged his foot behind the door until her friend left. He then dragged Beryl's body to the bedroom and covered it with an eiderdown. What to do? He would wait for the unsuspecting husband.

Timothy returned to be told that the 'operation' had gone badly – he would have to help Christie to dispose of her. This he did, helping him carry the body down to Mr Kitchener's empty flat. Christie assured him he would dispose of the body, down the drain. He would also look after the baby and make sure she would be adopted by a nice couple. All Timothy would have to say was that Beryl and Geraldine were in Brighton. Christie brilliantly manipulated the unworldly Evans, strangled baby Geraldine, and, on hearing of his sacking, suggested Evans leave for Bristol, or beyond. Christie assured him that Geraldine would be taken care of. He would also arrange for his friend, Mr Hookway, to buy the furniture.

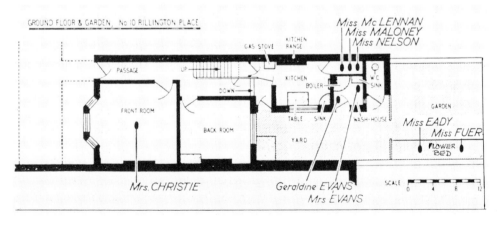

Plan of 10 Rillington Place.

Evans left London on the evening of Tuesday 15 November, after having visited Mrs Vincent. Christie put the bodies in the garden washhouse.

The tensions of the last two days, plus the heavy lifting, gave Christie a bad back for which he was treated. Meanwhile Evans turned up unannounced to his uncle's, Mr Lynch, in Merthyr Vale. They were pleased to see him but asked about his family. He relaxed for a few days, returning to London on 23 November, only to be turned back by Christie. The Lynches were suitably worried and wrote to his mother in London who, in turn, telegraphed Beryl's father in Brighton only to be told Beryl was not with him. Christie had also told them she had left on 8 November. Finally, after much heartbreak, Timothy turned himself in to Merthyr police station.

The garden at No. 10 Rillington Place.

He made two statements: the first to say he had killed his wife and put her down the drains (the London police checked, but the cover was too heavy for one): the second to explain about the abortion and that Christie had put Beryl down the drain. Christie said he would look after the baby and also told Evans to leave London.

The Notting Hill police checked the flat and the garden, finding a stolen case and a newspaper cutting about a torso murder in Evans's flat on 1 December – these had certainly been left there by Christie to incriminate Evans. They then requested Evans be brought back to London, where they interviewed him for three hours. They also interviewed Christie.

Another check on the house and garden finally revealed the bodies of Beryl and Geraldine behind some wood in the washhouse. Evans finally confessed to the two murders in his fourth statement, much to the relief of the police. All that remained was for him to be charged with the murder of his wife and daughter, and for his trial date to be set.

Evans wasn't helped by the prosecution using Christie as its prime witness, nor was he helped by the elderly lawyers he got on legal aid. He was also hampered by the fact that the police were not prepared to accept that the wood behind which the bodies had been found were only given to Christie on 14 November, despite being told this by the builders at several reprisals. If indeed Beryl had been 'left' on 8 November – that was the day she was killed. Her body and that of the baby would only have been moved on the 15th or after, when Evans was gone. The police were determined to make the charges stick no matter what the cost. None of Evans' statements, moreover, tallied with those of the builders. Dr Teare, the Home Office pathologist, also suggested that there might have been an attempt at sexual penetration at the time of death, but this was never to be brought up in court. Finally, the defendant's solicitor, Malcolm Morris, was only told of Christie's previous convictions just before the trial and therefore could not use this information.

Evans' trial began on 11 January 1950 and lasted three days. He was found guilty of the murder of his daughter, not his wife, and despite appeals was hanged at Pentonville on 9 March 1950.

The strain of the court case made Christie very ill. His weight plummeted and he was put on phenol barbitones by his accommodating doctor. The house was purchased by a Jamaican and Christie started a new job in September 1952, giving it up in December of the same year. Mrs Christie handed in her last laundry on 12 December 1952. She was never seen again, despite her relations receiving word from her in Mr Christie's handwriting.

A local prostitute, Rita Nelson, was last seen alive on 10 January 1953, as was another, Hectorina MacLennan, on 6 March. Finally Reginald Christie sub-let his flat on 16 March to an Irish couple, the Reillys, who were turfed out by the new landlord when he came to collect the rent. The landlord then allowed the new tenant of the top-floor flat to use Christies' kitchen. On cleaning it, the tenant discovered a papered-over alcove with the bodies of two trussed-up women, on 24 March.

This time the police took more time, finding Mrs Christie under the floorboards and two skeletons in the garden, one of which was headless. The hunt for Christie was on.

At about 9 a.m. on 31 March 1953, a policeman saw a man he recognised leaning over Putney Bridge. It was Christie! He was placed in Brixton Prison, where his obsessive neatness unnerved the other prisoners. Three doctors were to assess him. They all disliked him on sight and discovered that he always whispered when asked awkward questions, as if the loss of his voice would chase all bad things away. He made a statement to Chief Inspector Griffin, the man who had arrested Evans, confessing to the murder of seven people. He was quite candid about how much each death assuaged his blighted spirit, but never explained why he had to kill the baby.

His trial, for the murder of Mrs Christie, was held on 22 June 1953, before Justice Finnemore. The prosecution was led by Sir Lionel Heald and the defence by Derek Curtis Bennett. After a four-day trial the jury took just under an hour and a half to find him guilty and he was hanged on 15 July 1953.

It was too late for Timothy Evans. The lamb had been led to the slaughter and the police had only looked for results without bothering to look for the truth. The discovery of Christie's murders led to serious controversy – he admitted to killing Beryl Evans, which put Evans' guilt for the death of his own daughter in doubt.

For this reason, Evans was finally granted a posthumous pardon for the murder of his daughter in 1966, but he still remained implicated in the murder of his wife. It was only in 2003 that the independent assessor for the Home Office, Lord Brennan, accepted that Evans' conviction and execution was a miscarriage of justice.

This episode in the life of criminal investigation in Britain called for a massive overhaul of the judicial system and was one of the cases that led to the eventual abolition of capital punishment. It also called for an investigation into police criminal procedures, namely the overhaul of the interrogation system.

BIBLIOGRAPHY

BOOKS

Adam, Hargrave L., *Trial of George Chapman*, William Hodge and Co., 1930

Aronson, Theo, *Prince Eddy and the Homosexual Underworld*, John Murray, 1994

Begg, Paul, *Jack the Ripper: The Facts*, Robson Books, 1988

Birkenhead, Earl of, *Famous Trials*, Hutchinson and Co., 1925

Borowitz, Albert, *The Bermondsey Horror*, Robson Books, 1989

Caraman, Philip, *Henry Garnett, 1555-1606 and the Gunpowder Plot*, Farrar Strauss and Co., 1964

Carlin, Francis, *Reminiscences of an Ex-Detective*, Hutchinson and Co., 1925

Carswell, Donald, (ed.), *The Trial of Ronald True*, William Hodge and Co., 1925

Chester, Lewis, *The Cleveland Street Affair*, Weidenfeld and Nicolson, 1977

Downie, R. Angus, *Murder in London*, Arthur Barker, 1973

Eddowes, Michael, *The Man on Your Conscience: An Investigation of the Evans Murder Trial*, Cassell and Co., 1955

Evans, Stewart P. and Skinner, Keith, *The Ultimate Jack the Ripper Sourcebook*, Constable & Robinson, 2000

Fido, Martin, *Murder Guide to London*, Weidenfeld and Nicolson, 1986

Fido, Martin, *The Crime, Detection and Death of Jack the Ripper*, George Weidenfeld and Nicholson, 1987

Fletcher Moulton, H. (ed.), *The Trial of Steinie Morrison*, William Hodge and Co., 1922

Fraser, Antonia, *The Gunpowder Plot*, Arrow Books, 1999

Hodge, James H. (ed.), *Famous Trials 5*, Penguin Books, 1955

Jones, Steve, *When the Lights Went Down*, Wicked Publications, 1995

Kennedy, Ludovic, *Ten Rillington Place*, Victor Gollancz, 1961

Lane, Brian, *The Murder Guide to London*, Magpie, 1992

Loomie, Albert, *Guy Fawkes in Spain*, University of London, 1971

Macintyre, Ben, *The Napoleon of Crime*, Bantam, Doubleday, Dell, 1997

Marshall, Alan, *The Strange Death of Edmund Godfrey: Plots and Politics in Restoration London*, Sutton Publishing, 1999

McLaren, Angus, *Prescription for Murder: The Victorian Serial Killings of Dr Thomas Neill Cream*, University of Chicago Press, 1993

O'London, John, *London Stories*, T.C & E.C. Jack, Edinburgh

Parmiter, Geoffrey de C., *Reasonable Doubt*, Arthur Barker Ltd, 1938

Pillet, René-Martin, *Views of England during a Residence of Ten Years*, 1818

Rayner, J.L., and Crook, G.T., *The Complete Newgate Calendar*, Navarre Society, 1926

Read, Simon, *In the Dark*, Berkeley Books, 2006

Tennyson, Jesse, F., *The Trials of Timothy John Evans and John Reginald Halliday Christie*, William Hodge and Co., 1957

Walford, Edward, *Old and New London*, Cassell, Petter, Galpin & Co., 1904

Watson, Katherine D., *Dr Crippen*, National Archives, 2007

Young, Filson, (ed.), *The Trial of Hawley Harvey Crippen*, William Hodge and Co., 1920

NEWSPAPERS

The Chronicle, 19 July 1910

The Evening Independent, 10 June 1922

Lloyds Weekly Newspapers, 17 April 1892

The New York Times, 22 August 1910

The New York Times, 12 June 1922

Pall Mall Gazette, 24 March 1903

The People, 24 July 2010

The Times, 14 November 1849

The Times, 8, 28 May 1876

The Times, 17 March 1903

The Times, 7, 8, 9 and 10 March 1911

The Times, 16 July 1923

OTHER

The Cleveland Street Dossier, DPP1/95/1-7

Dictionary of National Biography

Egan, P., 'Account of the trial of Mr Fauntleroy for forgery', (1824)

Ryder, Stephen P. and Piper, John A., 'Dr Thomas Neill Cream – a Paper'

Trial Transcripts, John Bellingham

Williams, C.A.J., *Greenacre, or the Edgware Road Murder*, printed by Thomas Richardson, pamphlet

Other titles published by The History Press

Greater London Murders
LINDA STRATMANN

Greater London has been home to some of the most shocking murders in England, many of which have made legal history; this compendium brings together thirty-three murderous tales that made headline news across the country. They include George Chapman, who was hanged in 1903 for poisoning three women; lovers Edith Thompson and Frederick Bywaters, executed for stabbing to death Thompson's husband; and Donald Hume, who was found not guilty of the murder of Stanley Setty, but later confessed to killing him, chopping up his body and disposing of it by aeroplane.

978 0 7524 5124 4

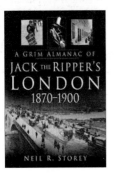

A Grim Almanac of Jack the Ripper's London 1870-1900
NEIL R. STOREY

Have you ever wondered what the London that witnessed the Jack the Ripper murders was really like? This almanac explores dreadful deeds, macabre deaths, strange occurrences and grim tales from the darker side of the capital's past. They include baby farmers, garotters, murderers, poisoners, prostitutes, pimps, rioters and rebels. This colourful cast of characters is accompanied by accounts of prisons and punishments, as well as a liberal smattering of funerals, executions, disasters and bizarre events. Read on, if you dare . . .

978 0 7509 4859 3

The Little Book of London
DAVID LONG

The Little Book of London is a funny, fast-paced, fact-packed compendium of the sort of frivolous, fantastic or simply strange information which no-one will want to be without. London's looniest laws, its most eccentric inhabitants, the realities of being royal and literally hundreds of wacky facts about the world's greatest city (plus some authentically bizarre bits of trivia), combine to make it required reading for visitors and locals alike.

978 0 7509 4800 5

Paranormal London
NEIL ARNOLD

From sightings of big cats such as the Southwark Puma and the Cricklewood Lynx to the terrifying tales of the Highgate Vampire and Spring-Heeled Jack, along with stories of mermaids, dragons, fairies and alien encounters, this enthralling volume draws together a bizarre and intriguing collection of first-hand accounts and long-forgotten archive reports from the capital's history.

978 0 7524 5591 4

Visit our website and discover thousands of other History Press books.
www.thehistorypress.co.uk